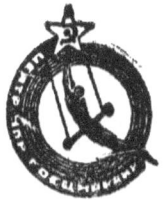

The Art of the Juggler: Exhibition Catalogue

Original print by Leningradskii Oblastlit, No. 3 314. Print run 2000-1 1/2 L. 16^0.

'Comintern' Printing House, 1 Krasnaia Street. Museum of Circus Publications. Authored by E.P. Gershuni

The original edition of this book, published in 1929 in Russian, has become public domain under both American and Russian law.

The copyrights of this 2018 English translation are by Niels Duinker. Printed in the United States of America by CreateSpace.

Book Translation: Helena K
Cover Image: Massimiliano Truzzi
Cover Design: Milos Zivkovic
Interior Design: Marijo Šarić

Special thanks to Juggling Archive Karl-Heinz Ziethen Berlin and Jessica Jane

ISBN-13: 978-1987453164
(CreateSpace-Assigned)

ISBN-10: 1987453166

Central Administration of State Circuses
Museum of the Circus and Variety Arts

The Art of the Juggler: Exhibition Catalogue

Leningrad
1929

Museum of the Circus

Establishing the world's first Museum of the Circus and Variety Arts in Leningrad is just one step along the road of Cultural Revolution to preserve the history. The other goal is to improve the skills and knowledge of those in the entertainment industry, especially the circus and variety performers.

It is impossible to create an authentic Soviet circus without studying its entire history over the course of many centuries.

A new generation of young Soviet circus and variety artists must be nurtured through a well-balanced blend of physical development and real spiritual culture.

The Museum of the Circus, established on the circus property itself, is not a portrait gallery of circus performers or a collection of various documents. It is a foundation that allows performers to study their craft and will enable visitors to learn about the circus and the different genres throughout history.

The Museum should serve as a basis for the further Sovietization of the circus and variety arts, and the adaption of an authentic culture by those who work in this industry.

At present, the activities of the Museum are focused on the following main areas:

1) Collecting materials on the history of our national entertainment, on the professional circus, professional variety shows and ultimately all materials that illustrate or reflect the everyday life of the circus and variety arts. Detailed records of all disciplines of the circus and variety arts make up a card catalog, organized both alphabetically and thematically.

The different categories of this card catalog are the history of the equestrian circus, the French Fight, the history of pantomime; variété and so on are kept separate. The depiction of the circus in children's literature, cinema, and theater also has a place in the Museum.

2) Cataloging and evaluating all these materials for the development and use of the Marxist methods in the sociological analysis of the history of the circus and variety shows.

3) Recording all circus routines (regardless of genre) through a specially developed system that will allow any routine to be reproduced in the future.

4) Establishing libraries that contain memoirs, research, historical texts, methodologies, etc., as well as fiction relating to all aspects of circus and variety shows.

5) Organizing regular exhibitions on various topics with materials taken from the Museum's collection on the history and everyday life of the circus and variety shows.

Two exhibitions already have taken place this year. The first dealt with the theme "Carnivores in the Circus," while the second looked at "The Training of Animals." A third exhibition that just opened and to which this catalog is dedicated is entitled "The Art of the Juggler."

The catalog is the first attempt to classify and categorize materials relating to the history of a single circus genre.

There may be mistakes, inaccuracies, and omissions in this work. These can partly be explained by the short time available for assembling this catalog, and partly by the fact that the museum's materials have not yet been sorted fully. The authors of the catalog will gratefully take feedback and bear it in mind for future projects.

The Museum of the Circus considers it its duty to thank the Central Administration of State Circuses, P.N. Scheffer, L.I. Zheverzheev and V.S. Protopopova from the Museum of Academic Theaters, the circus artists M.S. Paschenko, Massimiliano Truzzi and Victor Ferroni, members of the Organizing Committee E.P. Ivanov, B.P. Tamarin, and circus director Sarrasini, all of whom made this exhibition possibly through their advice, suggestions, and loans of exhibits.

E.P. Gershuni

THE ART OF THE JUGGLER

At present, we understand the term "juggling" to mean the art of throwing, catching and balancing objects. Juggling requires agility and rhythm of movement, a keen eye, control over one's body and the ability to get one's bearings quickly concerning falling objects to be able to catch them in time.

Different kinds of jugglers have different names: craft jugglers (i.e., strongmen jugglers), comic jugglers (who blend juggling skill with clowning), equilibrists (who combine juggling skills with acrobatics), and "ground" jugglers. "Ground" jugglers is what circus professionals call jugglers that carry out routines on the floor without heavy objects or a particular comic character.

Occasionally artists from other disciplines - circus riders and cyclists for example - will use juggling as part of their act to showcase the perfect mastery of their primary specialty and make their routine more varied. Finally, nearly all jugglers work with their feet while lying on their backs (antipodists) as well as working with their hands.

It is worth mentioning that jugglers rarely confine themselves to the categories above. Very often a juggler who has earned the title of craft juggler will also juggle with the lightest objects. For example, a peacock feather. Another juggler might present both comic and non-comic routines.

The objects that jugglers handle are varied: balls, sticks, canes, barrels, samovars and so on are all used. It is possible to juggle objects of the same size, shape, and weight (identical balls, sticks) simultaneously, and objects of different weights, proportion, and shapes (a ball, a bottle, and an egg). It is possible to perform one movement with one hand and another with the other hand (juggle plates with one hand and balance a spinning ball on a stick with the other) etcetera.

In general, no other circus discipline offers such variety or demands such a constant, prolonged, patient practice as juggling.

The current exhibition aims to show images of juggling in various countries at various times. The images either belong to the Museum of the Circus and Variety Arts or have been specially obtained for the exhibition from other institutions or private individuals.

The exhibits are divided into two sections:
I. Juggling in the ancient world, in the East, in the Middle Ages and the modern world up to the second half of the 19th century.
II. Juggling since the second half of the 19th century and up to the present day.

A. Ia. Andreev

I.
JUGGLING IN THE ANCIENT WORLD

Egypt gives us the most ancient evidence of jugglers. There are ancient Egyptian images that correspond perfectly to our contemporary ideas about juggling.

Exhibit number.

1. A depiction of a drawing on an ancient tomb: four women juggling balls. The juggling depicted is relatively complicated. One of the women is throwing the balls to two other women, one standing in front of her and the other behind her.

2. A depiction of a drawing on an ancient tomb: two women throw balls at each other while sitting on the backs of two other women that are bent over.

Juggling existed in Ancient Greece in as early as the 6th century BC, which is indicated by drawings on Greek vases that have been preserved. Moreover, we have the testimonies of Ancient Greek writers. For example, the writer Xenophon, in his description of a banquet hosted by a wealthy Greek, mentions a female dancer who would rhythmically roll, throw and catch 12 large hoops while dancing.

3. A depiction of a drawing on an ancient vase: a Greek dancer dances with a hoop.

4. A depiction of a drawing on an ancient vase: a juggler stands on one leg and balances a sharp-ended amphora (large jar) on the toes of his other foot.

5. A depiction of a drawing on an ancient vase: a woman does a handstand and juggles a tambourine with her feet (antipodist).

6. A depiction of a drawing on an ancient vase: a woman does a handstand. She balances a jar on top of a ball perched on the neck of a large amphora on the toes of one foot. With the toes of her other foot, she holds a spoon, which she obviously is about to use to help pour something from the amphora into the jar.

In Ancient Rome, jugglers mostly used small balls. Artists were called 'pilarius,' from the word 'pila,' which means ball.

7. A depiction of a drawing on an ancient

vase: a young man juggles seven balls, which nowadays is considered a significant feat.

Here, only the pilarius himself is depicted, but on the original vase, the surroundings are also visible – there are beautiful building and spectators of all ages.

Through the Greeks, we discovered that the art of juggling in India was extremely well developed. The historian Quintus Curtius notes that, during his India campaign, Alexander the Great (4th century BC) was shown a juggler who had perfected his art to such an extent that he could throw peas onto sharp distance needles without missing the target.

Unfortunately, we have no images of ancient Indian juggling.

8. Engraving from a printed publication: an Indian juggler with hoops depicted as part of a group of acrobats (around the middle of the 19th century).

The art of juggling was highly prised in Japan and took on unique, fantastical forms.

9. Engraving from Aimé Humbert's book, 'Japan Illustrated' (published 1870) – a juggler at a fair at the foot of a mountain range.

Edo-Asaksa. A special device for juggling: a cylindrical canister with holes to allow balls to roll to the ends, attached to a stick. Three cups are attached to small sticks that protrude from the canister. There are gaps between the sticks in the canister as well. It is being used to juggle two balls – they roll in the canister, balls are thrown out of one of the holes and caught in the cups.

10. Engraving from Aimé Humbert's book, 'Japan Illustrated' (published 1870) – Juggling on a false nose (sometimes replaced by a bamboo rod).

1) An acrobat with an artificial nose (in this case, bamboo) lies on his back on the floor, while a juggler clambers up it, balancing an umbrella on his nose, which is also artificial but smaller. In one hand, the juggler holds a fan, and with the other hand, he juggles five balls.

2) A juggler balances a hoop on his detachable nose and juggles balls through it.

11. Engraving from Aimé Humbert's book, 'Japan Illustrated' (published 1870) – Magician jugglers (juggling is seamlessly interwoven with magic tricks).

One of their routines features juggling with

spinning tops. A juggler takes two large spinning tops and starts spinning them. The other juggler picks up one of the spinning tops and lets it spin sideways along a pipe. He then throws the spinning top and catches it in a tube. Finally, he drops the spinning top to the floor. It then spins up an arched beam to a varnished table. The second spinning top spins on a lotus leaf floating in a bowl of water. The juggler makes small spinning tops pass through hoops, jump into a box and run across a wire or the edge of a saber. In the case of the second trick, the jugglers let the audience inspect the saber first, then secretly switch it for a different saber with a ridge running along the sharp edge.

Another routine involved the juggler cutting a piece of paper into small rectangles, throwing it in the air and hitting them with a fan. He would then turn them into a flock of birds in flight.

They had many complicated tricks like this. Of course, this kind of juggling requires a lot of apparatus – but even more so, agility and lightness of touch.

12. Engraving from Aimé Humbert's book, 'Japan Illustrated' – equilibrist jugglers.

A juggler balances a pole on his head, on the tip of which is a cup of tea covered by a saucer. He shakes the pole, so the tea spills out until the cup is empty.

We have no images of ancient Chinese juggling.

13. Lithograph with an image of Arr Hee. Chinese juggler who performed in London around the middle of the 19th century. Property of the Museum of Leningrad State Theatres.

14. (1 and 2) Photographs of a Chinese juggler from the Dzin-Tao troupe of jugglers and swordsmen. He is juggling with a stick with tridents on the end, making it roll down his body in different directions. The other artists are swordsmen.

15. Photographic portrait: a juggler from the Dzin-Tao troupe.

The name 'juggler' appeared in the Middle Ages and meant joker or jester. The first jugglers roamed from town to town and castle to castle, singing songs to praise the great deeds performed by heroes. But bit by bit, they began doing magic tricks, taming animals and, finally, showing off their dexterity by 'turning balls on their feet.' They would also juggler their weapons, which consisted of throwing, catching or balancing them.

16. Photograph from Lacroix's book, 'Mœurs, usages et costumes au moyen âge et à l'époque de la Renaissance' (Paris, 1877). Jugglers from the 13th century are balancing swords.

Foreign jugglers appeared in Russia in the 18th century.

17. Engraving – a poster for the 'English Company of Comedians', which visited Moscow around 1762-65. Property of the Museum of State Theatres.

The poster shows the exercises practiced by the Company's artists and explains exactly what they are doing. At the same time, 'a female character dances with ten drawn swords on a spot no larger than a plate. She did more than 2000 pirouettes in time with the music, while changing the position of the swords more than 40 times (placing them on her nose, eyes, lips, and chest without stopping).

18. A lithographic portrait of Angelo Orsini, who called himself the 'Indian juggler.' He performed in St. Petersburg as a twelve-year-old in 1826. He is pictured juggling knives in an elaborate Indian costume.

19. Photograph of a drawing on a poster:

strongman and juggler Carl Rappo, who was declared the 'Hercules of the modern day,' balances five wheels.

20. Photograph of a drawing on a poster: Carl Rappo juggles sabers, making a 'crown of sabers from them and balancing a replica of a sailing vessel.

21. Photograph of a drawing on a poster: Carl Rappo throws himself into the air from a column (to which his legs are fixed with some device) and assumes a horizontal position. He spins a stick using two other sticks.

22. Photograph of a drawing on a poster: Carl Rappo balances four cannonballs, one of which weighs 60 pounds, with the rest weighing 40 pounds each. He rests the cannonballs on his wrist and then rolls them across his shoulders to the other wrist.

He performed with his troupe in the St. Petersburg theatre-circus during several seasons, beginning in 1829.

Rappo is primarily remembered as a strongman, but in reality, he juggled with incredibly light objects (including a piece of burnt paper) as well as heavy ones. Another of his routines consisted of balancing a cannonball on his

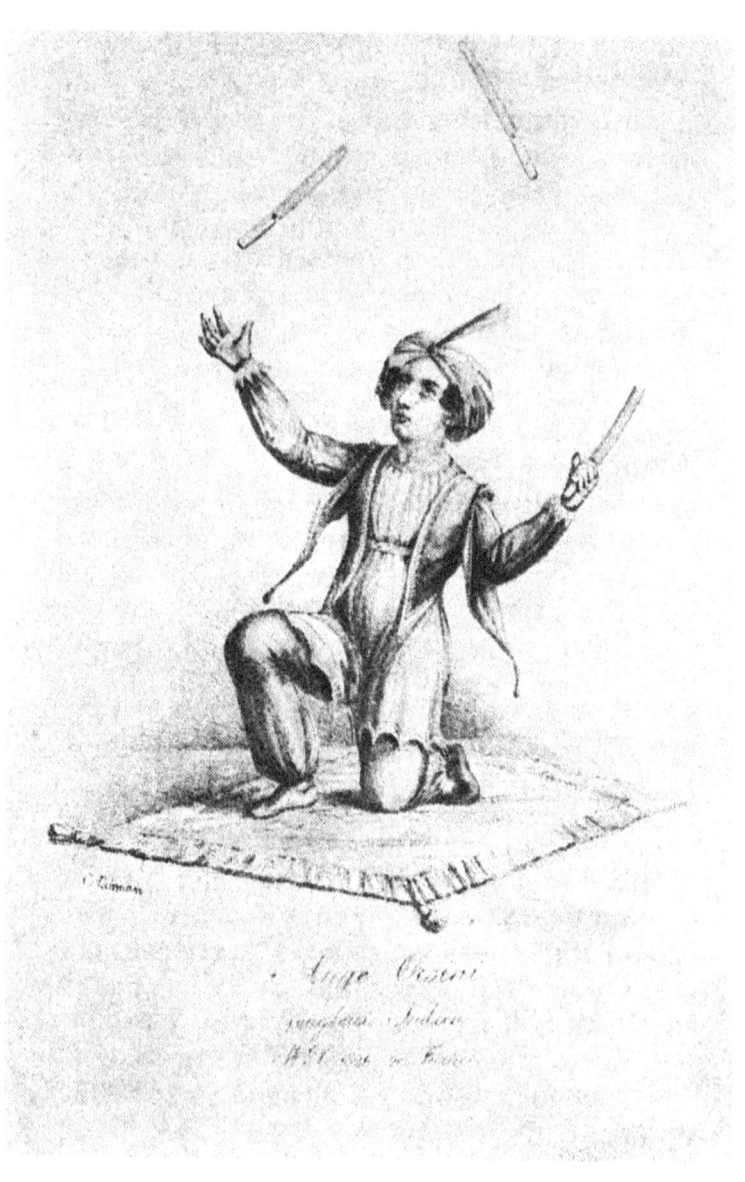

No. 18.

nose. On top of the cannonball was a Hercules' club (a club cast from lead), and on the tip of the club, there was a full glass of water. In general, like the majority of artists of that time, Rappo was not only a craft juggler, but also an equilibrist and vaulter, and would perform as both in the same performance.

23. Advert for the peasant Grigorii Ivanov from Vladimir province, dating back to around the 1830s – 1840s. Property of the Museum of State Theatres.

Ivanov declares that he will 'put a hat on his head using his foot, throws the hat in the air with his teeth and catch it on his head, throws the hat in the air with a stick and catch it on his head... the stick will spin on a needle, he spins the stick on the palm of his hand, stands it up on the opposite end and makes it dance on his palm, he balances one stick on top of the other...'

24. Photograph from a drawing on a poster: unknown juggler juggles three balls. Poster for a performance in the 'Maryina Roshcha' pub garden, four versts from Peterhof – 1838.

II.
JUGGLING UP TO THE PRESENT DAY

We have many more artifacts dating from the second half of the 19th century onwards. For this reason, and for the sake of clarity, we have organized our material according to the categories of juggler that were set out in the foreword.

It should be pointed out that, towards the end of the 19th century, the jugglers that were not content with the ordinary objects often tried to introduce the most unexpected items into their routines, objects that were seemingly least suited to juggling. So instead of using cannon balls, craft jugglers showed their strength and ability with cannons, cars and so on. Other jugglers swapped flaming torches for lit candelabras, samovars, and similar items. The aim was to draw attention, not so much to the art of juggling itself, but more to the objects that were being juggled.

a) CRAFT JUGGLERS

25. Photographic portrait: Jouanieré juggles a cannonball. Property of the Museum of Leningrad State Theatres.

26. Photographic portrait: Andreas Dollar juggles with missiles as well as cannonballs.

27. Advert: Hais Jensen juggles weights.

28. Autotype portrait (from an advertisement): an unknown man balances a cannon on his forehead. Property of E. E. Teviashev.

29. Copy of a drawing from the newspaper 'Hercules,' 1914: John Holtum, called the 'king of cannons.'

His first performance was in 1873. He juggled cannonballs, catching them on his biceps, chest and the back of his head. He then caught a cannonball that had been fired from a cannon in his hand (the cannon may have been specially adapted for this trick).

30. Cutting from an advertisement: Spadoni balances a car on his forehead. Property of E. E. Teviashev.

Not only did Spadoni repeat Holtum's trick with a cannon (see no. 29), he also made it even more difficult by catching the cannonball on the nape of his neck rather than with his hand. Furthermore, the cannonball weighed 175 English pounds. He invented a trick that involved a cannon being hoisted onto a retractable platform with a pulley on rails. When the cannon fell from the platform, Spadoni caught it on his shoulders and even walked a few steps under its tremendous weight.

31. Cutting from an advertisement: an unknown man catches a cannon on his shoulders as it falls down a slope. Property of E. E. Teviashev.

32. Cutting from an advertisement: Paul Conchas catches a set of cannonballs dropped from above on his shoulders. Property of E. E. Teviashev.

33. Cutting from an advertisement: Paul Conchas catches a landmine on his shoulders. Property of E. E. Teviashe.

34. Cutting from an advertisement: an unknown man performs two tricks. 1) Catching a missile on the back of his neck, and 2) balancing a cannon. Property of E. E. Teviashev.

35. Photographs: Rite and Knape (they later performed under the pseudonym 'David, Goliath and Ko').

36. Autotypes: 'David, Goliath and Ko' entering the ring.

37. Poster: Captain Andre balances a cannon.

38. Poster: Captain Johansen juggles cannon balls and balances a firing cannon and an anchor.

39. Poster: Captain Morro juggles life rings, catches landmines thrown from a trampoline on his shoulders, catches cannonballs thrown from above and balances a mine.

b) COMIC JUGGLERS

40. Photographic portrait: Mac-Turk.

41. Photographic portrait: Mac-Turk.

42. Visual advertisement for Mac-Turk's tricks. He performed at the Leningrad State Theatre in February 1926.

43. Photographs: Metz and Metz.

44. Visual advertisement for Metz and Metz's tricks. We have categorized jugglers that acted out whole sketches with a corresponding set as comic jugglers.

45. Photograph: 'Scene in a Parisian Restaurant,' the signature act of the clown-juggler Agoust, well known in Paris, and his troupe.

He appeared dressed as an old bon vivant accompanied by a lady. A waiter and a maître d' went about their work while juggling (not serving food, but throwing the objects they picked up to each other in an arc or circle through the air). Bit by bit, the elderly visitor, and his lady began following their example, and the whole stage was filled with flying objects: fruit, matches, glasses, etc.

This troupe performed at the Ciniselli Circus in St. Petersburg in 1895/6.

46. A Willy Pantzer poster.

47. Half-tone etching: 'Scene in a restaurant kitchen' performed by the Willy Pantzer troupe.

48. Cutting from an advertisement: the Perezoff Troupe on stage.

49. Advertisement for two Gervais tricks.

50. Advertisement for Robbi's tricks.

51. Advertisement for 2 Gervais tricks.

52. Photographs of Stefani.

53. Poster of Stefani.

54. Poster of Stefani.

55. Photographs: Repp and his partner in the sketch 'King Repp.'

56. Portrait of Repp dressed as a king, printed in ink.

57. Portrait of Repp in costume, printed in ink.

c) EQUILIBRIST JUGGLERS

58. Photographic portrait of 'Footit.' Property of the Museum of Leningrad State Theatres.

Footit was primarily a gymnast, but in 1868, at the Berg Theatre, he performed several times as a juggler in a routine named 'A juggler runs on a ball.'

59. Photographs of the Schäffer family. Property of A.A. Schulz.

The Schäffers were a family of jugglers who were famous at the end of the 19th century. Karl, the father, juggled with cannon balls (craft juggler); his oldest son, Sylvester, juggled with balls and knives and performed as an antipodist with a wooden log, panels, chairs and a table. He would put 12 wooden barrels on his feet, with positioned on top his younger brother, Sebaldus. Sylvester would throw the 11 lower barrels upwards and catch the twelfth barrel with his brother on his feet. The middle son, Severus, was a famous equilibrist juggler. The older daughter Sidonia juggled on a slackline. The younger daughter Susanna was a renowned antipodist and juggled a large, lit lamp with a lampshade, a wicker couch and an iron bed on which a married couple made of card, 'Sir and Lady Denis,' lay.

They visited St. Petersburg in 1875 and performed on an open stage at the Zoological Gardens.

60. Photographic portrait: Sylvester Schäffer. Property of A.A. Schulz.

61. Photographic portrait: Sidonia Schäffer. Property of A.A. Schulz.

62. Programs for a performance at the Zoological Gardens on the 20th June and 15th August 1875 in which the Schäffer family took part. Property of A.A. Schulz.

63. Photograph from Streli's book, 'Acrobatics and Acrobats': Severus Schäffer juggling cannonbals.

64. Copy of a drawing from Streli's book, 'Acrobatics and Acrobats': Severus Schäffer. You see how Severus holds himself in a plank position in the center of a semicircular stand with six wooden barrels. With one hand, he spins himself on the neck of a jug on a small table, and with the other hand, he turns the barrels on the stand without stopping.

65. Copy of a drawing from Streli's book, 'Acrobatics and Acrobats': Severus Schäffer – four stages of a somersault with a large metal ball.

66. Photograph from Leroux's book, 'Les jeux du Cirque et la vie foraine': Severus Schäffer – trick with a lamp.

67. Photographic portrait: Joseph Blank.

68. Photographic portrait: Joseph Blank.

69. Photographs of Joseph Blank and his partner.

Blank supports his partner on the soles of his feet. His partner juggles four plates while balancing an object on her forehead.

70. Advertisement from the Spadoni agency: Joseph Blank and his troupe performing three tricks.

71. Photographic portrait: Mary Blank.

72. Photographs: the Langer troupe.

73. Photographs: the Langer troupe juggling hoops.

74. Photographs: the Uessem troupe juggling hoops.

75. Advertisement: the E. and M. Kyun troupe juggling hoops.

76. Photograph: an artist from the 4 Philips troupe juggles six plates while bouncing a ball on his forehead.

77. Photograph: the 4 Philips troupe juggles plates as a group. At the same time, one of the artists is balancing a large ball on his feet.

78. Photograph: the 4 Philips troupe juggles as a group. An antipodist juggles four plates while balancing a barrel on his feet. Another artist stands on the barrel with a third artist on his shoulders, who juggles four plates.

79. Advertisement: Alfred Fabri performing his tricks.

80. Advertisement for the Rikkert Brothers - images from several moments during their routines.

d) 'SALON' JUGGLERS

81. Copy of a drawing from Streli's book, 'Acrobatics and Acrobats': a trunk (a pedestal for antipodists, either standing on the floor or on top of a pole, which is attached to the floor with cables.) – Image of a routine on a trunk on a pole.

Balls, barrels or Maltese crosses were usually juggled on trunks. All these objects were hollow and very light. They were juggled incredibly quickly, so the Maltese cross, for example, would lose its shape and appear to be a solid, glittering circle.

82. Page from an album of circus drawings by Heinrich Lang: sketch of a hat with a peacock feather being juggled. Property of the Museum of Leningrad State Theatres.

83. Autotype from an advertisement: an unknown juggler works with three balls and six peacock feathers. Property of V. Ya. Andreev.

84. Copy of a drawing from Streli's book, 'Acrobatics and Acrobats': Cinquevalli balances a plate, a riding crop and a hoop.

85. Copy of a drawing from the same book: Cinquevalli balances a goblet, billiard balls, and a cue.

86. Copy of a drawing from the same book: Cinquevalli kicks a ball upwards, which then lands in a cup attached to his head.

87. Photographic portrait: Antonio juggles nine plates. Property of V. P. Lachinov.

88. Photographic portrait: Antonio with a device for balancing and juggling balls in one hand and a stick in the other. Property of V. P. Lachinov.

89. Photographic portrait: Antonio balances a piece of apparatus with balls on top on his forehead. He holds a stick in his teeth which he will use to catch the balls. Property of V. P. Lachinov.

90. Autotype image from an advertisement: a juggler with large spinning hoops. Property of E. E. Teviashev.

91. Photographs: 2 Bramson – jugglers spinning large hoops.

92. Photographic portrait: Emile balancing a plate on a stick. He has props around his feet: sticks, balls, and plates. Property of the Museum of Leningrad State Theatres.

93. Photographic portrait: Emile juggling three balls with one hand and holding a glass in the other hand to catch the balls with. He has props around his feet: sticks, balls and plates of various sizes. Property of the Museum of Leningrad State Theatres.

94. Photograph: the Bramsons juggling electric hoops. They performed at the Leningrad Circus Music Hall in December 1928.

95. Autotype image from an advertisement: unknown jugglers – group juggling with large hoops. Property of E. E. Teviashev.

96. Autotype image from an advertisement: unknown jugglers – group juggling with small hoops spinning on taut wires. Property of E. E. Teviashev.

97. Autotype image from an advertisement: group juggling with small hoops. Property of E. E. Teviashev.

98. Page from an album of circus drawings by Heinrich Lang: a sketch of juggling with a rubber ball. Property of the Museum of Leningrad State Theatres.

99. Photographic portrait: Emile. Property of the Museum of Leningrad State Theatres.

100. Photographic portrait: Emile balancing a place on a stick. He has props around his feet: sticks, balls, and plates. Property of the Museum of Leningrad State Theatres.

101. Photographic portrait: Emile juggling three balls with one hand and holding a glass in the other hand with which to catch the balls.

101-a) Photographic portrait of Kara.

101-b) Portrait of Kara (trick with small balls that are rolling down slanted ledges with holes in a cabinet) and his article, 'Myself and Juggling' ('Circus' journal, no. 15, 1926).

Michael Kara was the creator of the 'salon' genre. His routine took place on a restaurant set. He came in dressed in a tailcoat and monocle. He threw his coat, top hat and walking stick onto a coat stand, and put his monocle in his pocket. A chair, bottles, and glasses spun through the air before falling into their places. Above his head, a knife, fork, and apple would spin. While in the air, the knife cut the apple to pieces, which then threaded themselves onto the prongs of the fork. His artistry was so great, and his hands were so dexterous, that he could juggle three balls with his eyes closed.

102. Autotype image from an advertisement: an unknown juggler next to a cabinet with slanted ledges meant for juggling balls. Property of E. E. Teviashev.

103. Photographs: Mikhail and Kseniia Pashchenko. Mikhail S. Pashchenko is one of the oldest Russian jugglers. Property of Pashchenko.

104. Photographic portrait: Kseniia Pashchenko in costume. Property of Pashchenko.

105. Photographic portrait: Mikhail Pashchenko juggles balls on the floor.

106. Photographic portrait: Kseniia Pashchenko in costume by a table with props: plates and balls. Property of Pashchenko.

107. Photograph: M. Pashchenko stands in the middle of tables and stands with props.

108. Photograph: Mikhail and Kseniia Pashchenko by tables and stands with props.

109. Photograph: M. and K. Pashchenko by tables and stands with props.

Exhibits 107-109 are highly characteristic of the end of the 19th century - two tables and two sets of shelves, draped in decorative tablecloths and flags, are weighed down under objects of every possible kind. Even those that seem completely unsuitable for juggling - washbasins, different types of lamps, axes, and even a samovar with a teacup balanced on top. In short, everything imaginable that could astonish audiences and grab their interest.

110. Advertisement: the Pashchenkos – pictures of husband and wife and their tricks.

111. Advertisement: pictures of M. Pashchenko, images of various moments in his routines, and his props.

112. A replica of an exhibition of props used by a juggler at the end of the 19th century: a table with M. Pashchenko's props.

113. Poster for M. Pashchenko.

114. Cutting from an advertisement: Karl Lantini juggling an umbrella, a glove, and a top hat. This is an example of juggling with three objects that are completely different in size and shape.

115. Photographic portrait: Knok in costume.

116. Photographic portrait: Valentina Knok.

117. Photograph from an ink drawing by the artist I. Miasoedov depicting the work of the Knok couple.

118. Autotype portrait: Mikhalini (jubilee publication for the 40th anniversary of his artistic career).

119. Photographic portrait: Mikhalini.

120. Mikhalini's props: four small lamps.

121. Mikhalini's props: wooden sticks.

122. Mikhalini's props: two gilded wooden goblets.

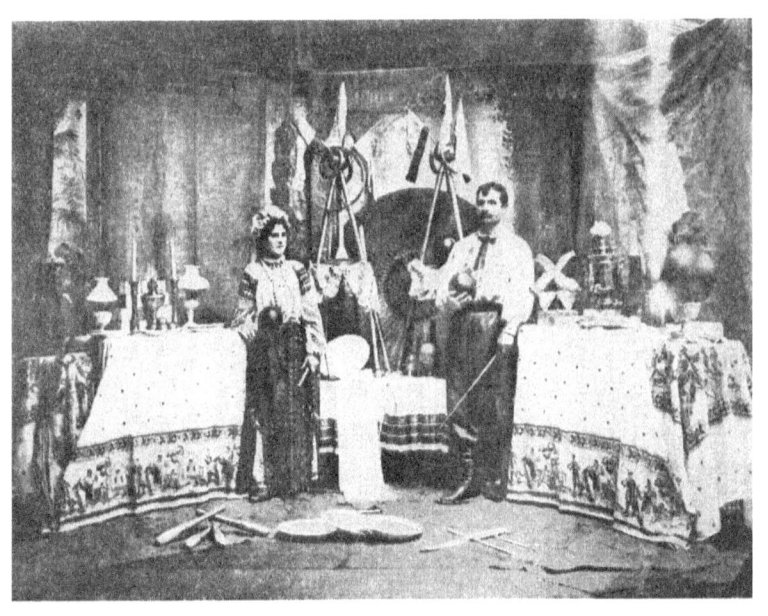

No. 108.

123. Mikhalini's props: device consisting of a lampshade supported by six ledges. A candelabra with four candles and a small lamp are balanced on top of it.

124. Poster for Mikhalini.

125. Photograph: Willy Jaeger and Mikhalini by tables with their props.

126. Advertisement: Willy Jaeger – a representation of his tricks. Property of V. Ia. Andreev.

127. Copy of a drawing from a promotional publication ('Organ', 1913): Willy Jaeger and two examples of a balance.

128. Advertisement: Wilhelm Jaeger – picture of his tricks. Property of V. Ia. Andreev.

129. Advertisement: Minin – picture of his tricks. Property of V. Ia. Andreev.

130. Cutting from an advertisement: an unknown juggler juggles candelabras. Property of E. E. Teviashev.

131. Cutting from the newspaper 'Das Programm': Jenny Jaeger.

132. Advertisement: Jenny Jaeger – picture of her tricks (balancing six hoops, ten balls, triple balance).

133. Photograph: Lizette and Janto – images of various moments from their routines and pictures of the artists. Property of V. Ia. Andreev.

134. Advertisement: M. and B. Berno juggle billiard balls.

135. Photographic portrait: Mme Berno with a cue in her hand.

136. Poster '2 Asra': jugglers on a billiards table. Asra juggled with balls in such a way that they hit the surface of the billiard table, bounced off it and fell on the trigger of a gun tied to the forehead of his wife, who was riding a bike around the billiards table.

137. Advertisement: the Ivanovich brothers juggle balls.

138. Photographic portrait: Anita Bartling.

139. Photographic portrait: Anita Bartling.

140 Advertisement: Anita Bartling juggles balls and torches.

141. Advertisement: Geraldo and Gerda juggle balls, hoops, and hats.

142. Photographs: 3 Ernesti.

143. Advertisement: 3 Ernesti juggling with hats.

144. Photograph: 3 Cartella and Vizhu juggle top hats.

145. Advertisement: 4 Ferdini juggling with luminous hats.

146. Poster for Miss Mary Kremser – antipodist.

147. Advertisement: Miss Mary Kremser, antipodist, juggles a chair, a screen panel, a bed, a table, a suitcase and a lit lamp with a lampshade. Property of V. Ia. Andreev.

148. Cutting from an advertisement: an unknown female juggler juggles balls.
Property of V. Ia. Andreev.

149. Photographic portrait: Pepi Vergan balances a small table on a three-legged stand

on her forehead. There is a vase of flowers on the table. Property of V. Ia. Andreev.

150. Poster: 3 Kronetz.

151: Poster: the Kronetz Sisters.

152. Flyer: Anatolii Codanti – pictures and printed reviews.

153. Letterhead featuring images of Anatolii Codanti's tricks.

154. Poster for Anatolii Codanti.

155. Autotype portrait: Takashima, a Japanese juggler of balls and sticks.

156. Poster for Takashima.

157. Photographs: the Rastelli family.

The Rastellis are a family of circus artists; the father is a juggler and gymnast, the mother is a horseback rider and the son, Enrico, is the famous juggler who brought about a revolution in contemporary juggling by bringing it back to its classical roots. A fairly prolonged stay in Japan allowed him to get acquainted with the

Japanese school of juggling – juggling with wooden sticks and balls. He decided that he too would specialize in this kind of juggling, but introduced some changes by swapping specially made cloth balls for ordinary rubber balls. In contrast to the colorful, diverse props that used to be fashionable among jugglers, Rastelli works with simple props. He has brought about a return to classical juggling and prefers to draw attention to simple juggling technique.

158. Phototype portrait: Enrico Rastelli balances three balls.

159. Phototype portrait: Enrico Rastelli balances balls on sticks on his forehead and in between his teeth.

160. Phototype portrait: Enrico Rastelli balances balls on his feet, his shoulders and a stick.

161. Phototypes: Enrico Rastelli and Max Hansen.

162. Cutting from the German newspaper 'A.I.Z' (no. 40, 1928): Enrico Rastelli – images of three of his exercises.

163. Photographic portrait: Massimiliano Truzzi.

On a par with Rastelli, Truzzi is a brilliant representative of classical juggling and has an exquisite mastery of the most complicated movements and rhythms. He borrowed some tricks from the Japanese (with balls and sticks), and others from Rastelli, but developed many tricks himself.

164. – 168. Photographic portraits: Massimiliano Truzzi.

169. Photograph: M. Truzzi juggles six plates while spinning a hoop with his right hand. Property of L. Truzzi.

170. Photograph: M. Truzzi balances balls on his foot, the nape of his neck and a stick held between his teeth. Property of L. Truzzi.

171. Photograph: M. Truzzi balances two balls on his foot, one on each knee and one on a stick held between his teeth.

172-1. Photographic portrait: M. Truzzi balances balls on his foot, on his head, and he balances two balls on a mouth stick.

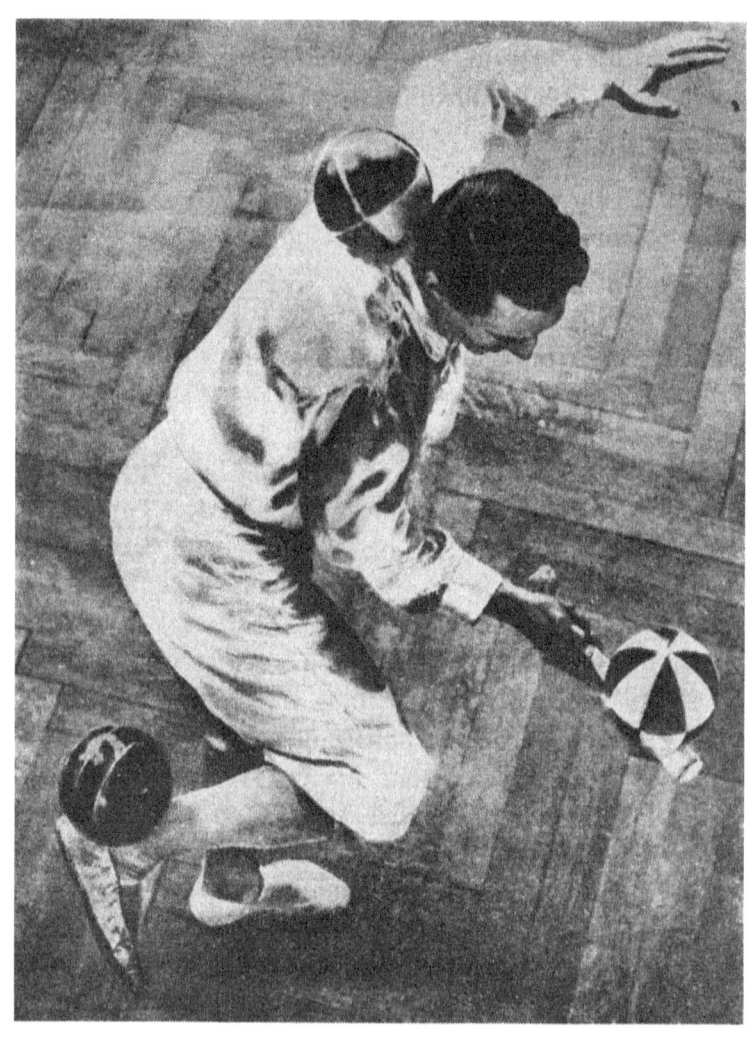

No. 160.

172-2. Photographic portrait: M. Truzzi balances balls on his head and knee. He also balances two balls, with a balance stick in between them on a stick held between his teeth, and two balls on a stand on his toe. The upper ball is not in shot.

172-3. Photograph: M. Truzzi balances balls on his head and knee and two balls, with a balance stick in between them, on a stick held between his teeth. He balances a ball with a little stand and another ball on top of his foot. He also balances balls along with his arms.

173. Autotype portrait of M. Truzzi who is balancing balls. The article, 'A Pea and 13 Balls' ('Circus and Variety' journal, no. 7, 1928).

174. Cue sheet for M. Truzzi's routine compiled by A. D. Avdeev and A. A. Barten. This is a copy of the Museum of the Circus' first attempt at recording a circus routine. It gives a detailed description of the routine and its sequences.

175. Diagram of the audience's reaction to M. Truzzi's routine at the Kazan State Circus (work of the experimental theatrical workshop).

176. Cue sheet for M. Truzzi's routine compiled by A. D. Avdeev and A. A. Barten.

This is a copy of the Museum of the Circus' first attempt at recording a circus routine. It gives a detailed description of the routine and its sequences.

177. M. Truzzi's props – a ball.

178. M. Truzzi's props – a stick.

179-1. Indian ink drawing for a poster of M. Truzzi.

179-2. Poster of M. Truzzi.

180. Autotype portrait (cutting): Paolo Piletto balances balls on his feet, head and a stick held between his teeth (horizontally).

181. Autotype portrait (cutting): Paolo Piletto balances two balls on his forehead and a ball on a stick held between his teeth (vertically).

182. Advertisement for the Berlin Wintergarten (January 1928) – on the cover is a painted portrait of Paolo Piletto balancing balls on his forehead and a stick held between his teeth (vertically).

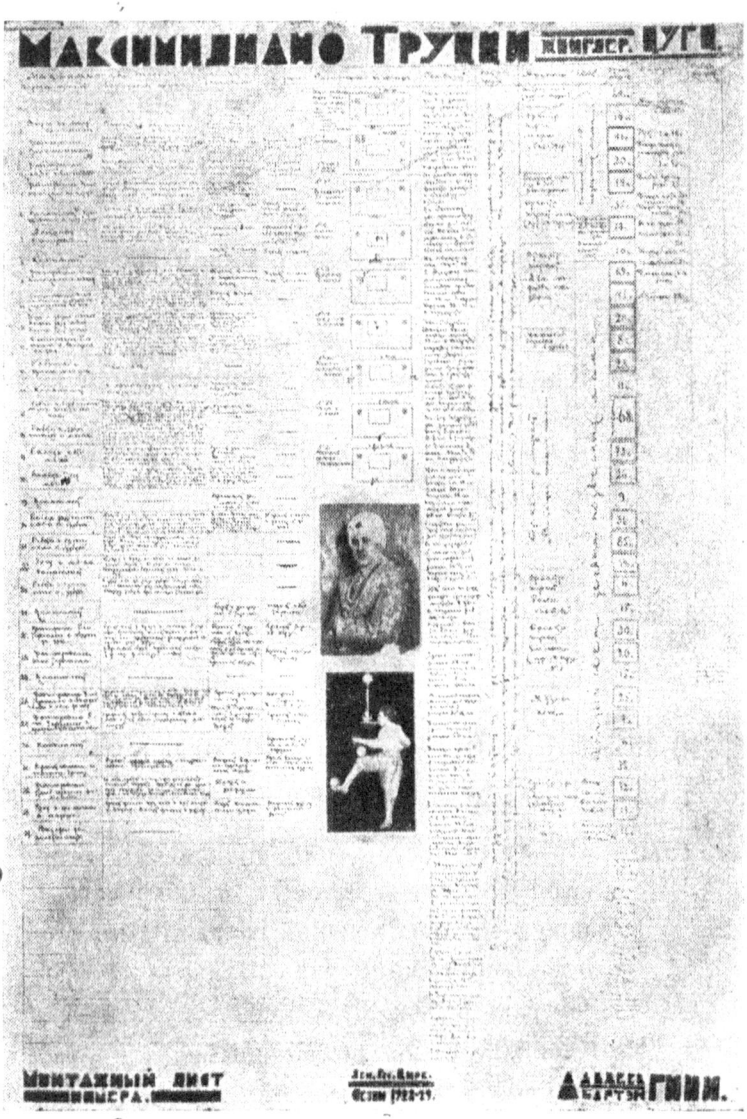

No. 176.

183. Photographic portrait: an artist from the Andos troupe balances balls on his head, horizontally on a stick between his teeth, on his knee, and on his toe.

184. Cutting from a German publication: two portraits of Bob Ripa. In one portrait he is balancing two sticks with balls on his forehead, a stick with a ball in his teeth (vertically), a ball on his toe and juggles six plates. In the other portrait he is balancing a ball on his head, balls on top of his wrists, on his knee, below his knee, on his toe and two balls with a stick between them on a stick between his teeth.

185. Cutting from the newspaper 'Das Programm': portrait of Jean Florian balancing a ball on a stick between his teeth.

186. Cutting from the newspaper 'Das Programm': portrait of Jean Florian balancing a ball on his cheek.

187. Advertisement – photograph: Gedi Vendini juggles torches, hoops, and balls.

188. Poster 2 Williams.

189. Poster 2 Eglit.

190. Poster of Felix Kario, an Indian juggler.

191. Poster of Killiani and Annette.

192. Poster of Tamara Blok, a female juggler, and illusionist.

193. Poster of Tamara Blok, a female juggler, and illusionist.

194. Poster of the Silvestri troupe.

195. Poster of Larry.

196. Photographic portrait: Kathi Gultini.

e) JUGGLERS WORKING ON HORSEBACK AND BICYCLES etc.

197. Announcement in Moscow 'Vedomosti' (no. 20, 1830) for the first drum major of the former Napoleonic Guard – Henri – and his great concert on the 10th March 1830. With drawings.

'During battle, he throws 26 drumsticks from 15 drums upwards, then balances them, moving forwards and backward in time to the music.'

198. Copy of a drawing from Streli's book, 'Acrobatics and Acrobats': the acrobat O'Cabe does a handstand on one hand on a rotating plinth. With his other hand he juggles three balls.

199. Copy of a drawing from the same book: image of a routine on a trunk on a pole – juggling large balls.

200. Page from an album of circus drawings by Heinrich Lang: sketch of a juggler juggling balls and balancing plates on horseback. Property of the Museum of Leningrad State Theatres.

201-1. Photographic portrait: Enrico Truzzi on the horse 'Minion' at the Yaroslavl Circus.

201-2. Photographic portrait of Enrico Truzzi.

202. Photographic portrait of Enrico Truzzi. Property of L. Truzzi.

203 – 206. Photographic portraits of Victor Ferroni. Property of V. Ferroni.

207. Program for Victor Ferroni's debut performance as a juggler on horseback in 1909. Property of V. Ferroni.

208. Watercolor sketches: Victor Ferroni:

1) juggles torches on horseback,
2) bounces a ball on his head on horseback while playing the guitar, and
3) his portrait. Property of V. Ferroni.

209. Watercolor drawing: Victor Ferroni juggles torches on horseback. Property of V. Ferroni.

210 – 211. V. Ferroni's props – two metal plates. Property of V. Ferroni.

212 – 213. V. Ferroni's props: two metal balls. Property of V. Ferroni.

214 – 215. Ferroni's props – two wooden sticks of different shapes. Property of V. Ferroni.

216. Ferroni's props – a leather head strap with a metal cup for catching balls. Property of V. Ferroni.

217. V. Ferroni's props – a leather head strap with three wooden candlesticks for catching candles. Property of V. Ferroni.

218-1. Photographic portrait of N. A. Nikitin. Property of V. E. Herzog.

218-2. Photographic portrait of N. A. Nikitin.

219. Advertisement: New Year's greetings with a portrait of N. A. Nikitin. Property of E. N. Bezkrovnaia.

220. Photographic portrait of Niko Nikitin. Property of V. E. Herzog.

221. Photographic portrait of Niko Kisso. Property of V. E. Herzog.

222. Photographic portrait of Borisov. Property of V. E. Herzog.

223. Photographic portrait of Flora Bemeth. Property of V. E. Herzog.

224. Advertisement: the Briatore brothers – their portraits and images of two of their tricks:

   1) juggling torches on horseback;
   2) a comic exit.

225. Portrait in oil: an unknown female artist juggler four balls on a slackline.

226. Advertisement: a portrait of Vilius and images of his tricks (on a wire).

227. Photograph: the Georg Narov troupe of cyclists juggle hoops on bicycles.

228. Photograph: the Georg Narov troupe of cyclists juggle bottles on bicycles.

229. Poster of the Georg Narov troupe.

230. Advertisement: Tilly and Dolly Price – tango jugglers.

231. Cutting from an advertisement: unknown equilibrists juggling balls.

232. Poster of the 'steel Voynitsky sailors' juggling on a pole.

233. Poster 3 Gogini – juggling with bottles on a ladder.

234. Photographs: the Illeroms troupe – jugglers balancing on a large ball.

235. Poster 2 Gartons – balancing and juggling.

236. Cutting from the newspaper 'Das Programm': a portrait of Miss Damur.

237. Poster of Yoki-San juggling on a trapeze.

f) MISCELLANEOUS

238. Program for a course in the art of juggling by the Moscow School for the Circus Arts.

239. Chinese woodcut – a game with a 'diabolo' which closely resembles juggling.

240. Reproduction of a painting by A. Gutschenreiter, 'The Wandering Artist'.

241. Shot of a statuette by Comene, 'Female Juggler'.

242. Painting of a juggler standing on a large ball and juggling bottles, plates and eggs at the same time.

243. Illustrated open letter with drawings of a female juggler working with three balls.

244. Cutting from the journal, 'Le Théâtre': a portrait of the artist Maréchal playing the juggler Jean in Massenet's work, 'Our Lady's Juggler', based on a story of the same name by Anatole France. He is juggling three balls.

245. Italian dish with an image of a juggler. Property of the Museum of Leningrad State Theatres.

246. Statuette of a juggler.

g) FINAL EXHIBITS

247. Photograph: Charles Eter with his props. Property of V. P. Lachinov.

248. Photograph: Charles Eter by a pyramid for equilibrists. Property of V. P. Lachinov.

249. Photograph: Charles Eter performs as an equilibrist on a pyramid made from four rows of gradually tapering bottles. He balances three plates on a head strap, two plates on each hand and a plate on each foot. Property of V. P. Lachinov.

250. Advertisement: the Sazonov troupe.

251. Poster of Jenny Jaeger.

252. Autotype portrait: Severus Schäffer.

253. Photographs: Joseph Blank and his partners.

254. Poster of Enrico Rastelli.

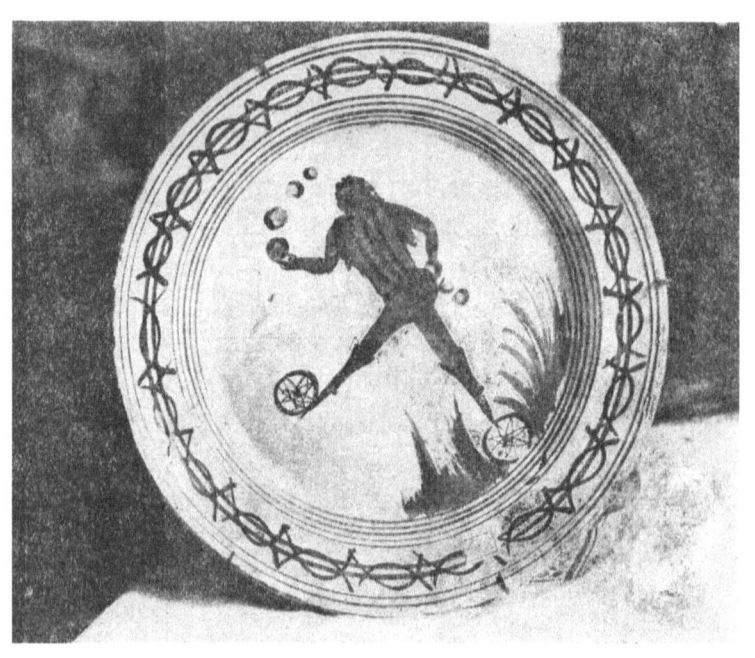

No. 245.

255. Photographs – advertisement: picture of N. A. Nikitin and his trick with torches on horseback.

256. Photographic portrait: Alfred Fabri balances seven balls.

257. Photographic portrait: Morgunov juggles four balls. This juggler was a member of the first graduating class of the Moscow School of Circus Arts.

258. Photographic portrait: an artist from the Andos troupe balances three balls.

259. Photographs: the Wallastons.

260. Photographic portrait: Marguerite Woodward.

261. Advertisement: Marguerite Woodward.

This book has been published by Niels Duinker

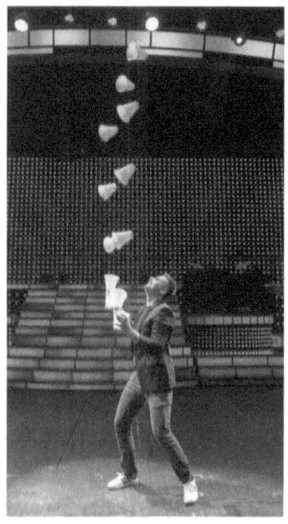 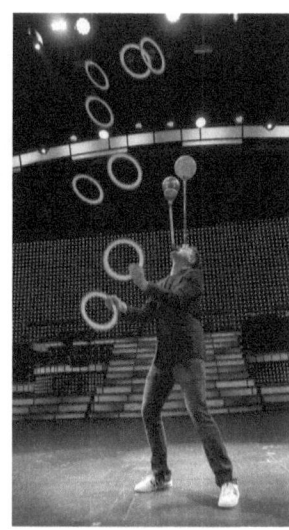

Niels Duinker (born 9 August 1985) is a professional juggler from Rotterdam in The Netherlands. He is a lifetime member of the International Jugglers' Association. Niels began his career in the youth circus of Rotterdam Circus Rotjeknor, and he has been mentored by Freddy Kenton and Daniel Holzman.

Niels now holds 7 Guinness World Records and has performed in theaters, on television, on cruise ships, and at events all over the world. Niels was the first and only person so far to do 14 juggling shaker cups.

He holds a Bachelor's degree in Mechanical Engineering from the Delft University of Technology in the Netherlands and won the Gold Medal at the 2009 circus festival in Taipei, Taiwan.

Niels has a passion for the history of juggling. Other projects he has been involved in are the translation and publishing of these other juggling books:

- *"Juggling, The Past and Future"* by Karl-Heinz Ziethen, 2017. ISBN 978- 9082167641
- *"Here's to You, THE JUGGLERS"* by Paul Adrian. Original book published in French, 1977. Translated into English in 2018. ISBN 978-1979802765
- *"If You Are a Juggler"* by Alexander Kiss, 2018. ISBN 978-1979653404
- *"Learn to Juggle: And Perform Family-Friendly Comedy Routines"* by Niels Duinker, 2017. ISBN 978-1546308683
- *"Catching Greatness"* by Niels Duinker, 2014. ISBN 978-9082167610

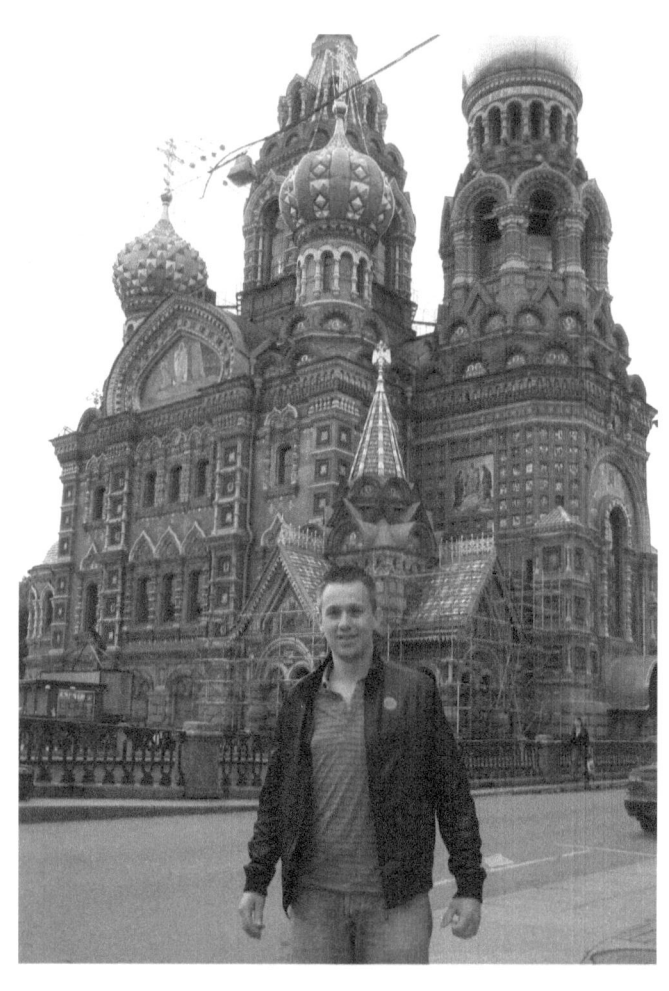

Niels Duinker in Saint Petersburg
(previously Leningrad), Russia

APPENDIX

Photos from the Juggling Archive
Karl-Heinz Ziethen.

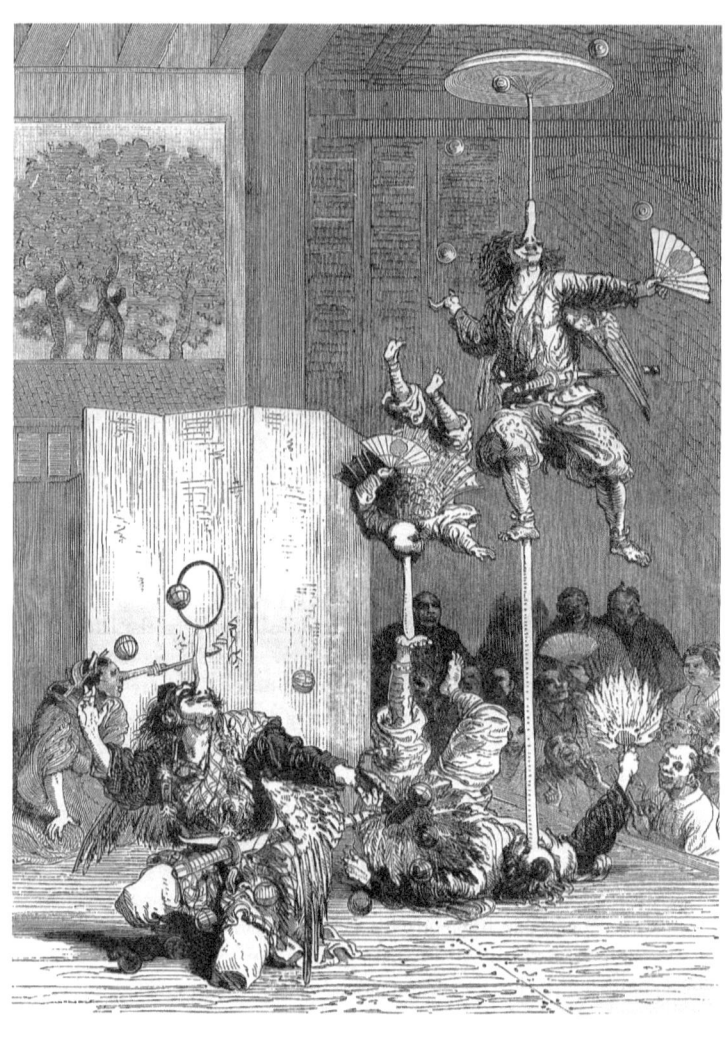

Engraving from Aimé Humber's book, 'Japan Illustrated'

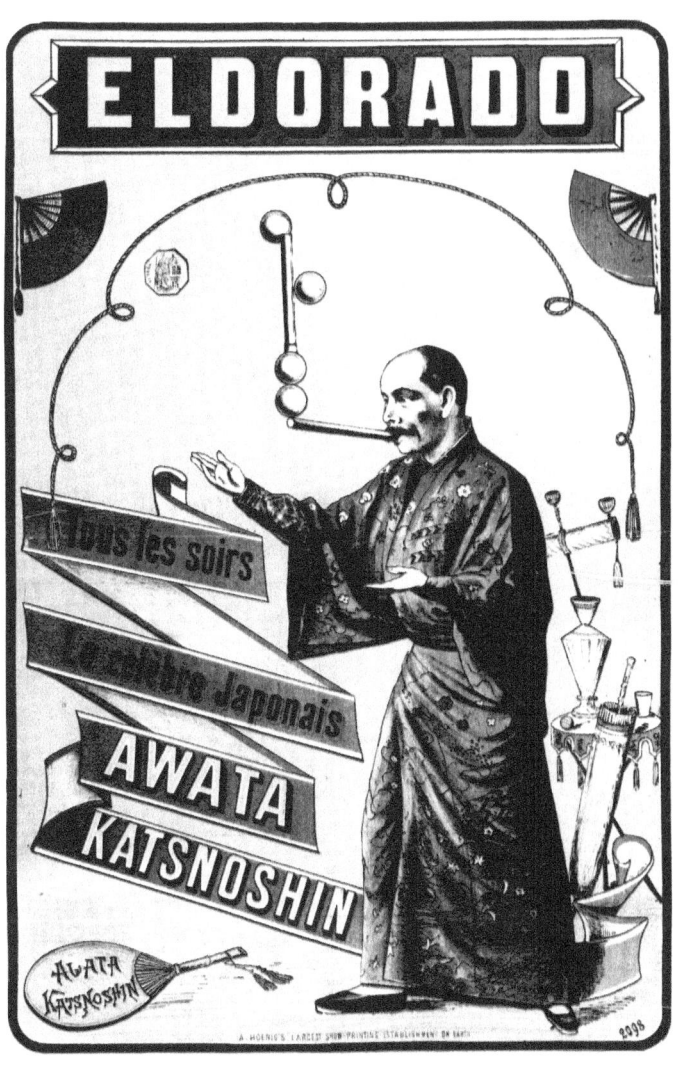

Awata Katsnoshin

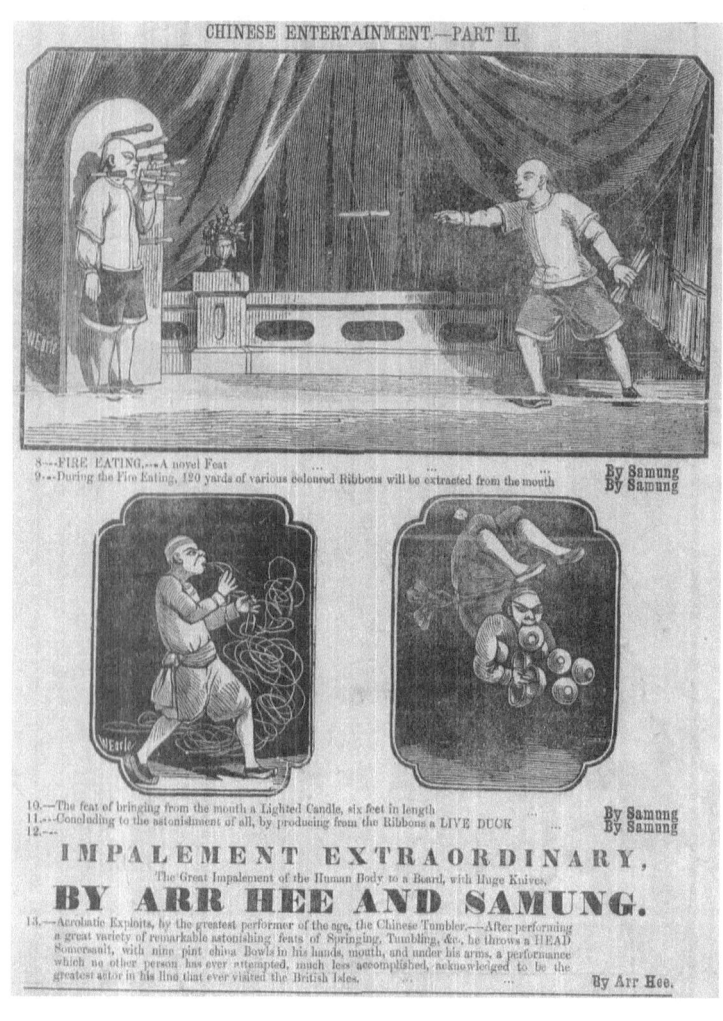

Lithograph with a mention of Arr Hee

THE GREAT ORIGINAL
CHINESE
ENTERTAINMENT,

From Drury Lane Theatre, (all others being imposters,) accompanied by

SIGNOR ZAMEZOU AND FAMILY.

TOWN HALL CONCERT SOCIETY.

GRAND JUVENILE CHRISTMAS ENTERTAINMENT.

FOR ONE NIGHT ONLY,

VICTORIA HALL, LEEDS,

Saturday, December 20th, 1862.

As performed before Her Most Gracious Majesty the Queen and the Royal Family!!

The Managers, in announcing the celebrated Chinese Jugglers,

ARR HEE,
SAMUNG, AND CHING FONG,

From the Celestial Empire, trust that they will receive that encouragement which has been so liberally accorded them in the Metropolis, where they appeared for 300 successive nights with immense applause, at Drury Lane. During the evening Arr Hee, the director of the Troupe, will perform the extraordinary feat, which has astonished all London, of IMPALING A MAN ALIVE!!

SIGNOR ZAMEZOU
and Family, from the Crystal Palace, in their celebrated
DRAWING-ROOM ENTERTAINMENT

CHINESE ENTERTAINMENT.—PART I.

1.—The Magic Balls ... By Arr Hee
2.—A Bowl of Water, containing one gallon, produced out of a shawl.—In performing this feat, which surpasses in ingenuity and skill anything previously accomplished, no machinery or collusion whatever is employed ... By Arr Hee
3.—A Large Wooden Ball, with two handles, performing various evolutions ... By Arr Hee
4.—Magic Cup.—A most singular and amusing performance, the cup actually broken, and to the astonishment of the audience, found whole again on the top of Samung's Back ... By Arr Hee
5.—Swing a Bowl of Water.—The Bowl is swung ten feet in the air, rebounding around the neck, arms, and various parts of the body, without spilling a drop ... By Arr Hee
6.—Handkerchief turned to a Pigeon, and the Pigeon to a Handkerchief ... By Arr Hee
7.—Flying Knives, with Fan ... By Arr Hee

Lithograph with an image of Arr Hee

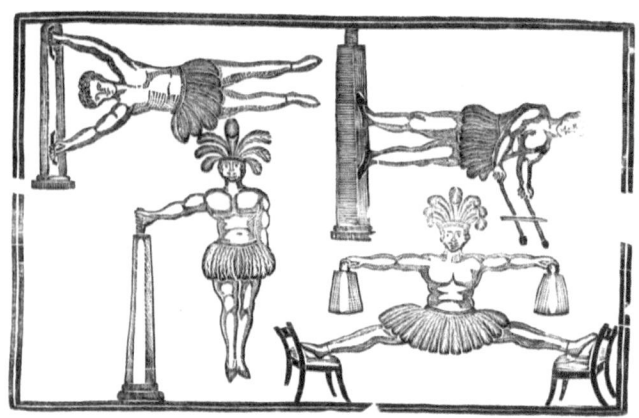

Carl Rappo

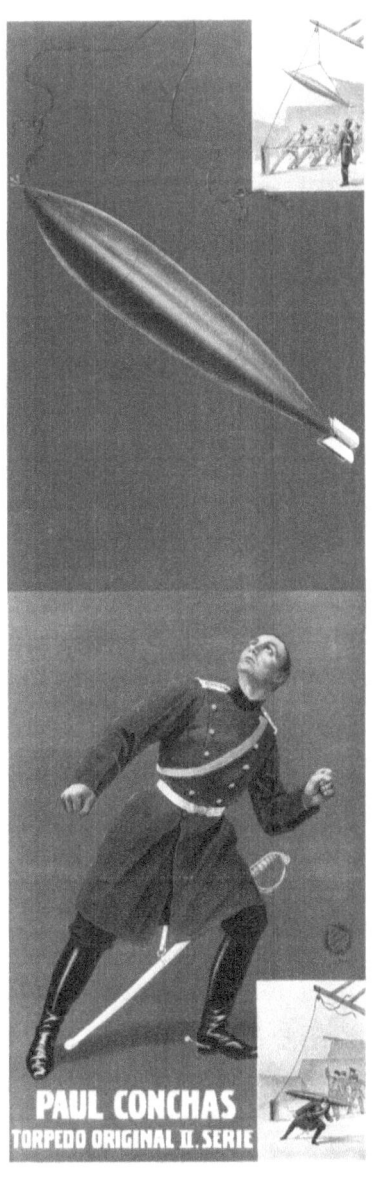

Paul Conchas

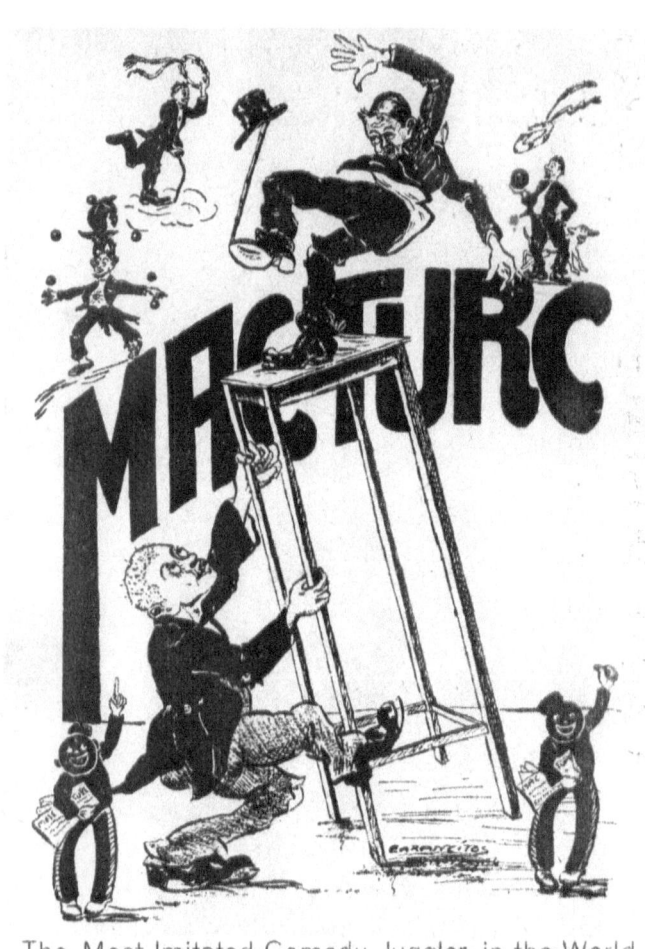

The Most Imitated Comedy Juggler in the World
from
Scala Berlin ——— Wintergarten Berlin

Mac Turc

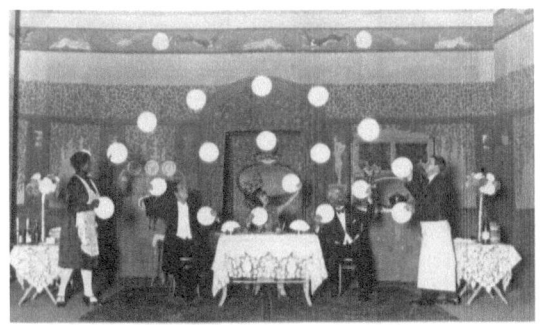

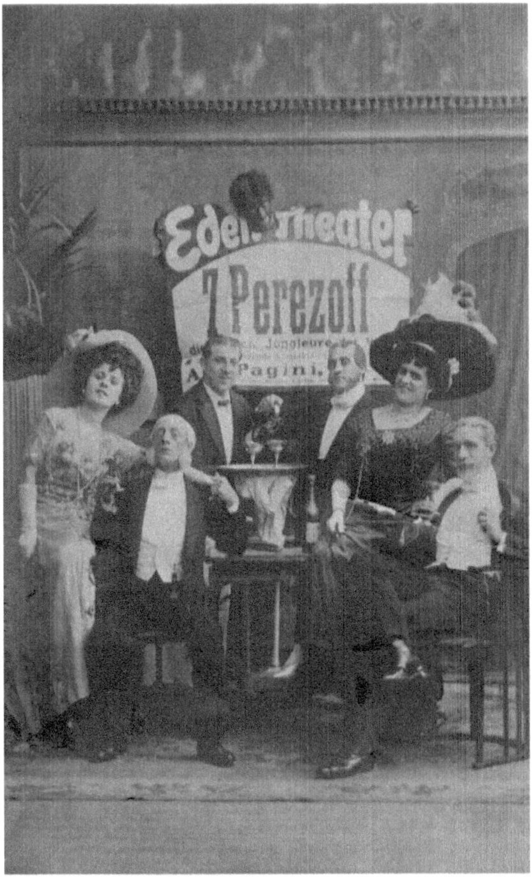

7 Perezoff

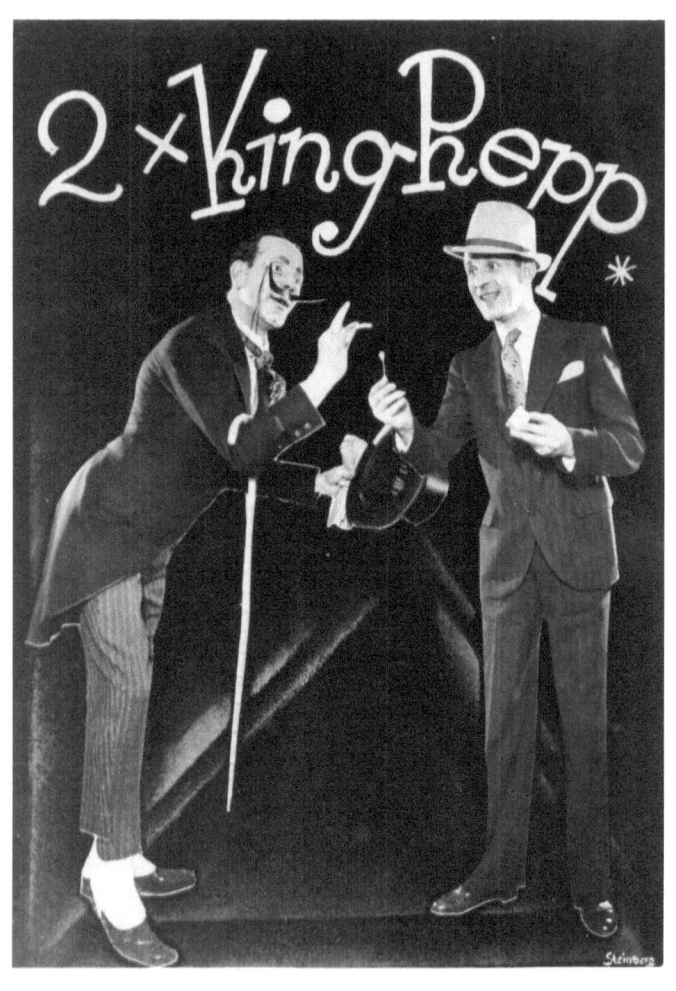

King Repp

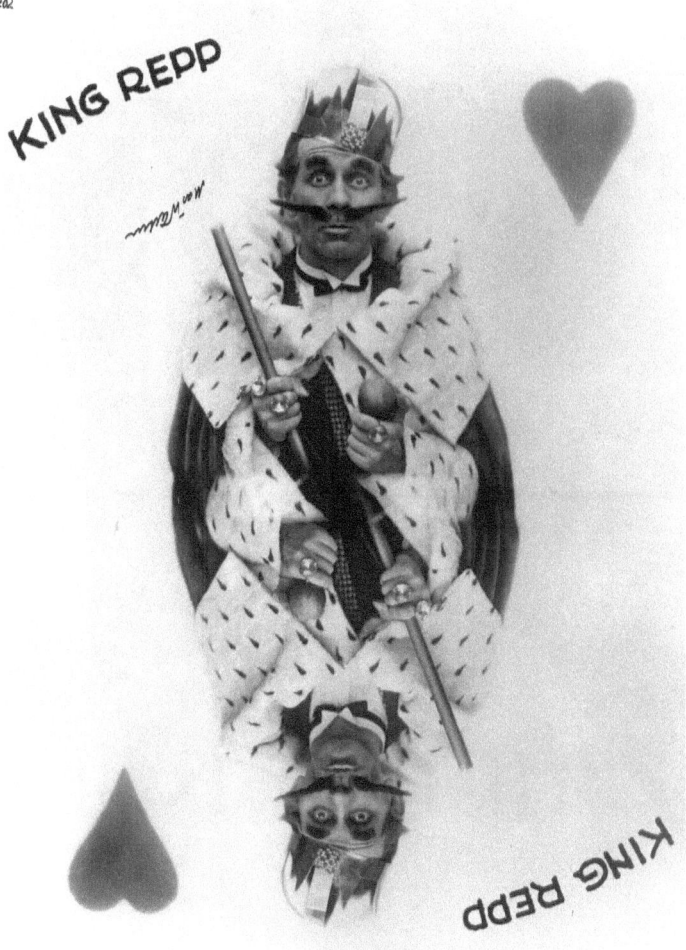

King Repp

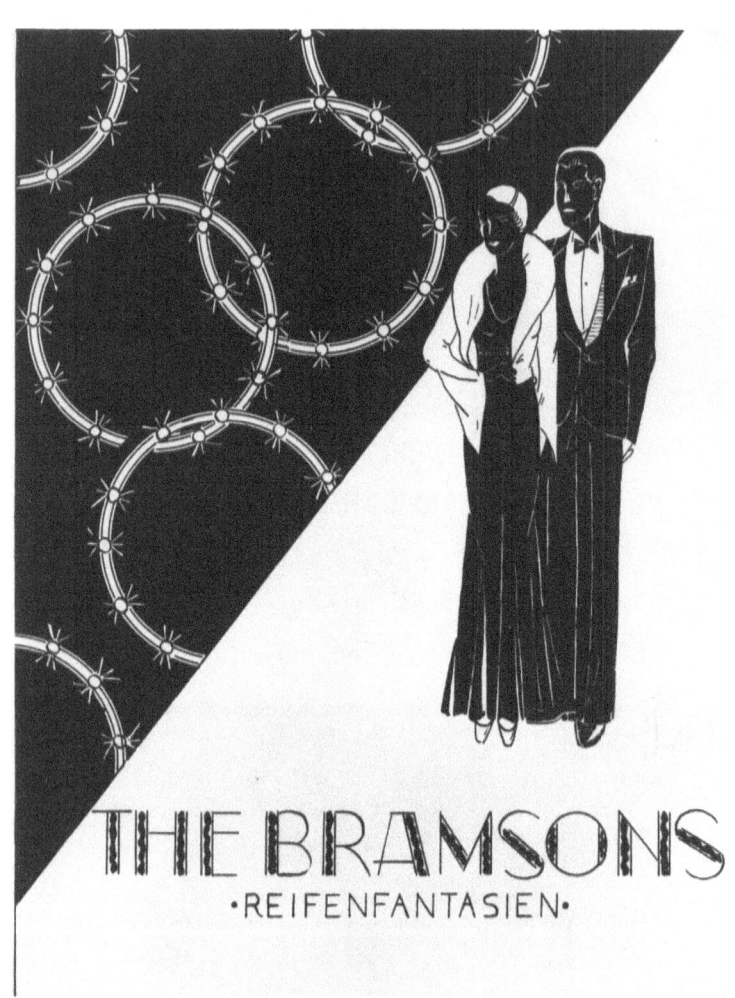

The Bramsons

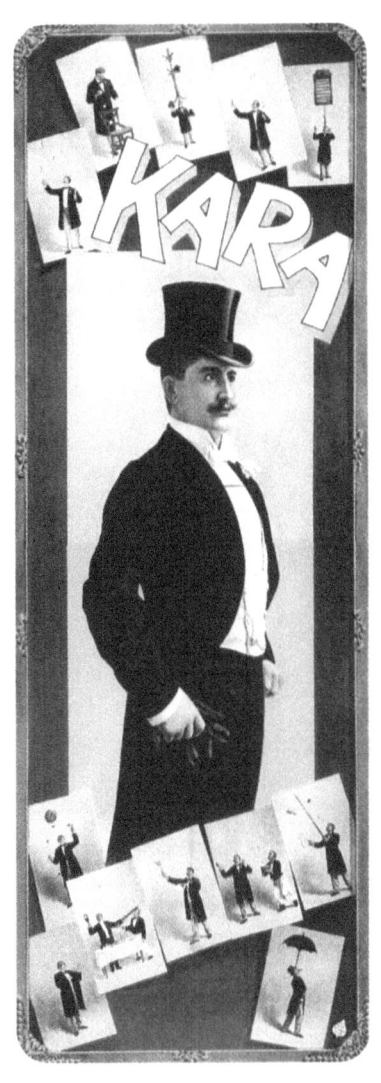

Michael Kara

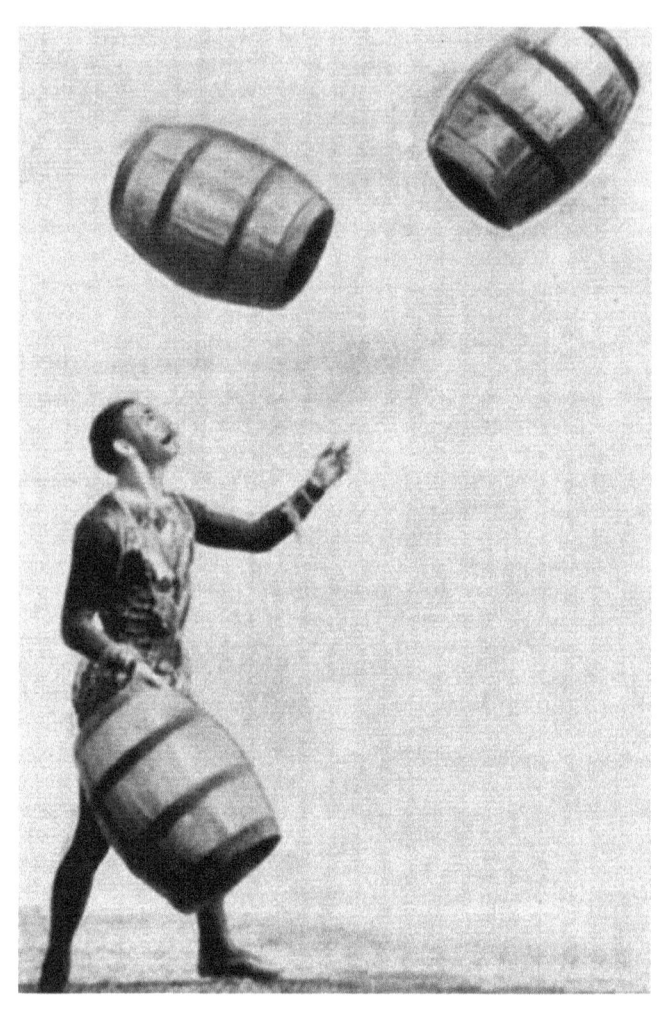

Paul Cinquevalli

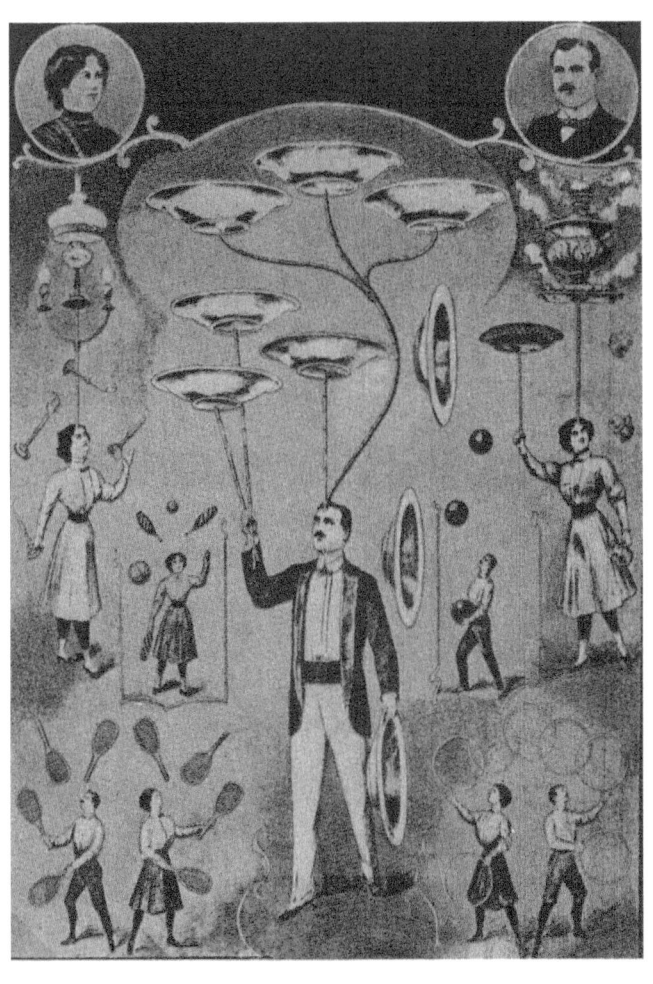

Mikhail (Mickael) Paschenko and Xenia

ВИЛЛИ ЕГЕРЪ

ЕДИНСТВЕННЫЙ, ВНѢ КОНКУРРЕНЦІИ УНИВЕРСАЛЬ-МАЛАБАРИСТЪ.

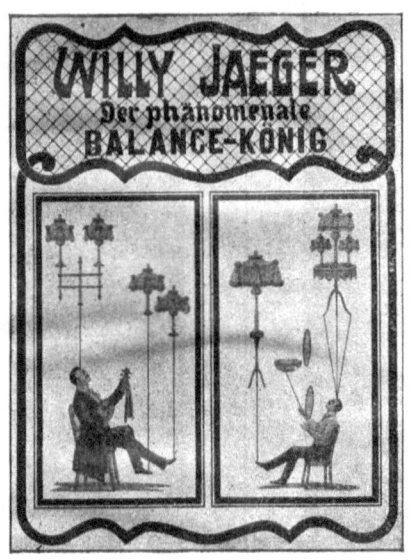

Въ доказательство вышеприведеннаго **1000 марокъ** тому, кто предлагаю исполнитъ мою работу.

Сейчасъ: Доблeнъ, электро-театръ.

Свободенъ съ 1-го декабря.

Пост. адр.: ред. ж. **„Органъ"**-

(156)

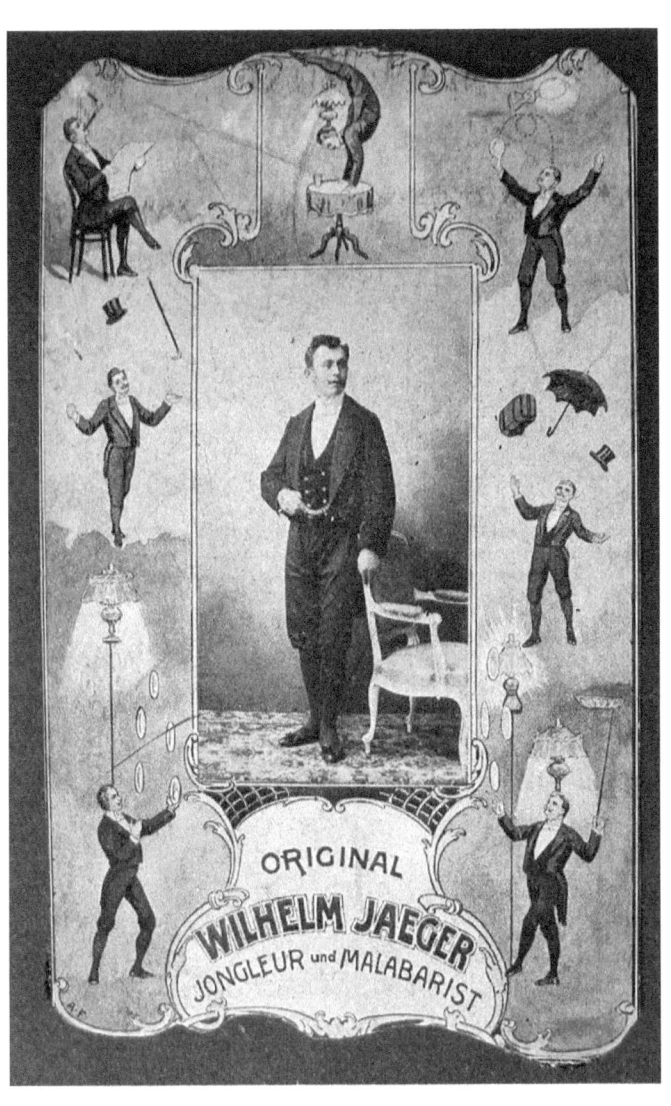

Wilhelm Jaeger

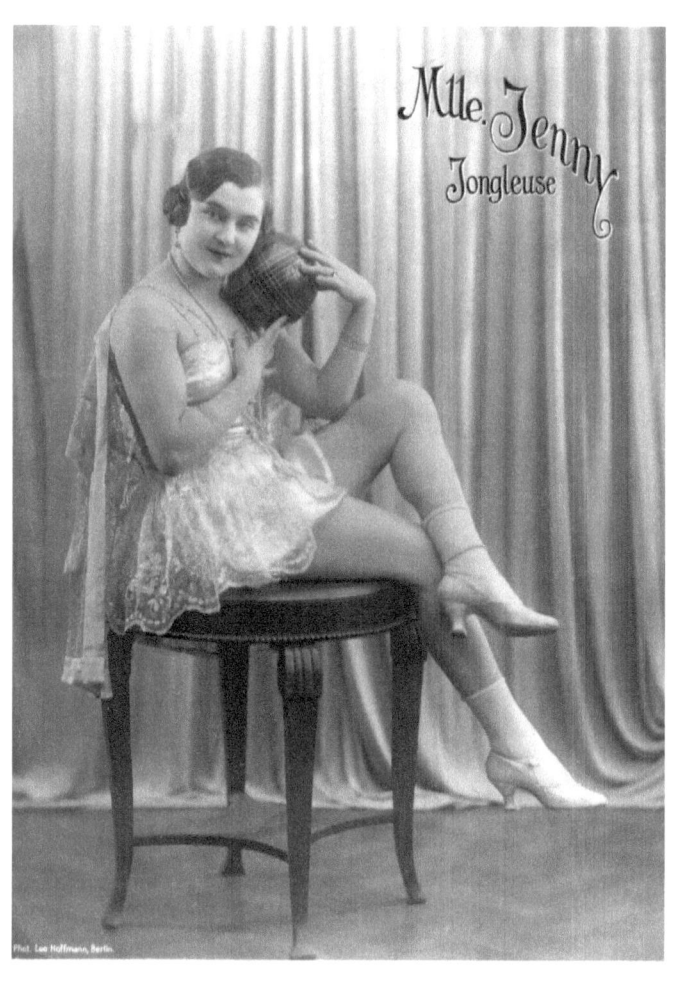

Jenny Jaeger

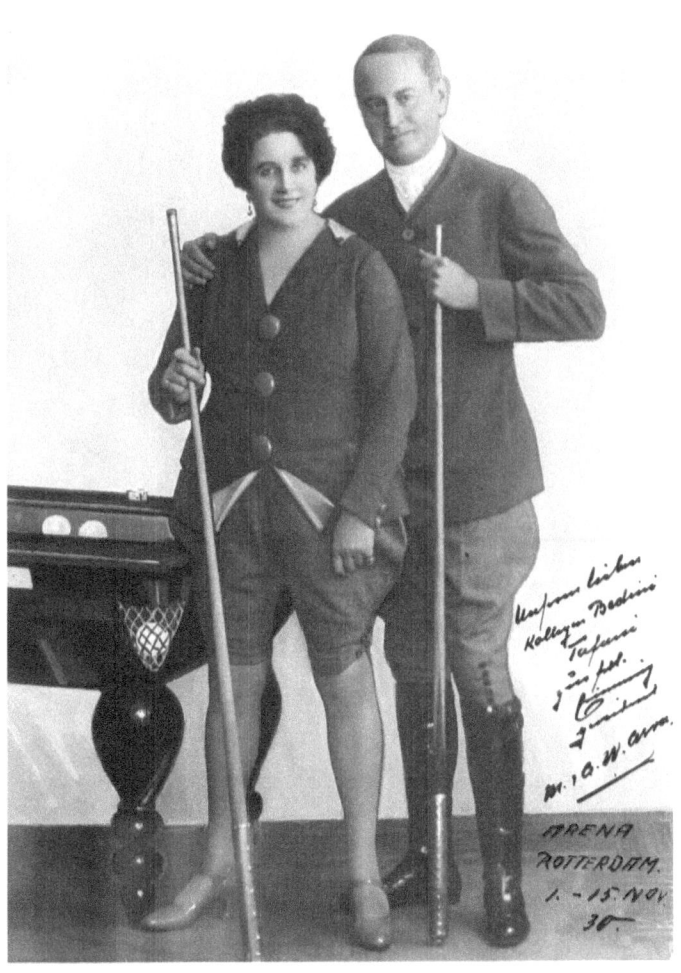

2 Asra

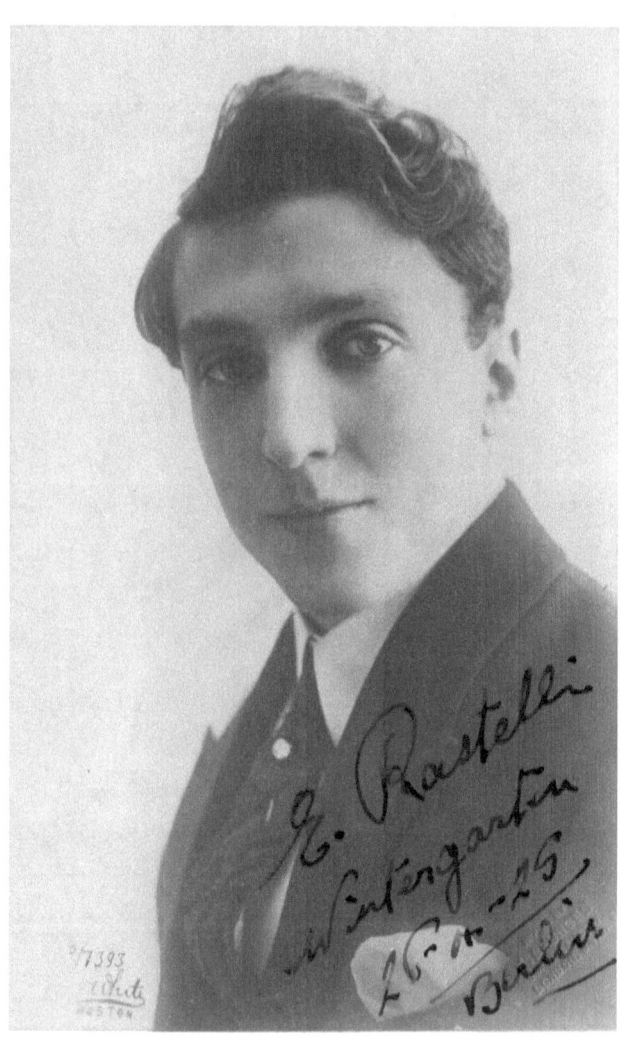

Enrico Rastelli

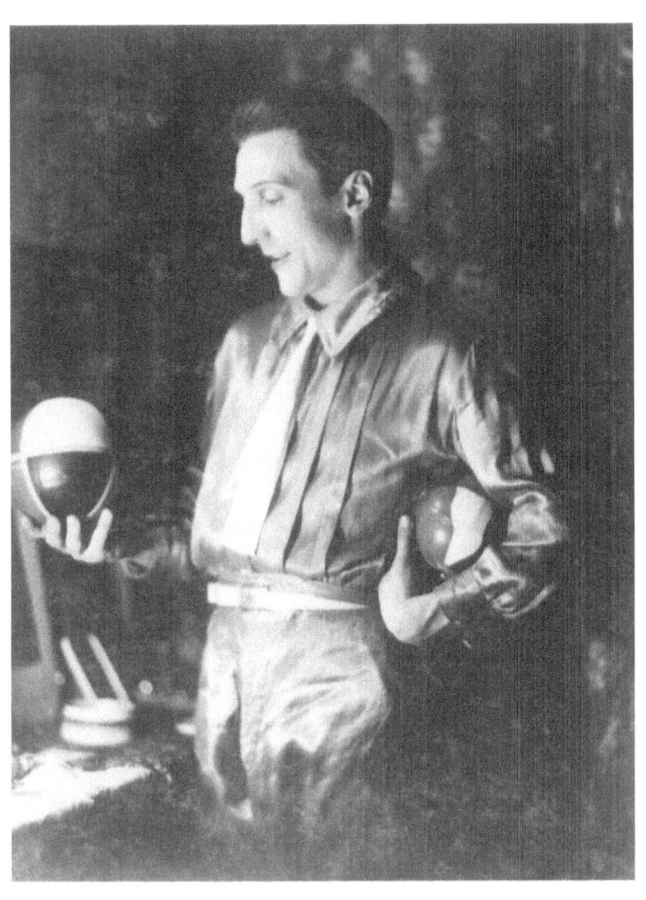

Enrico Rastelli

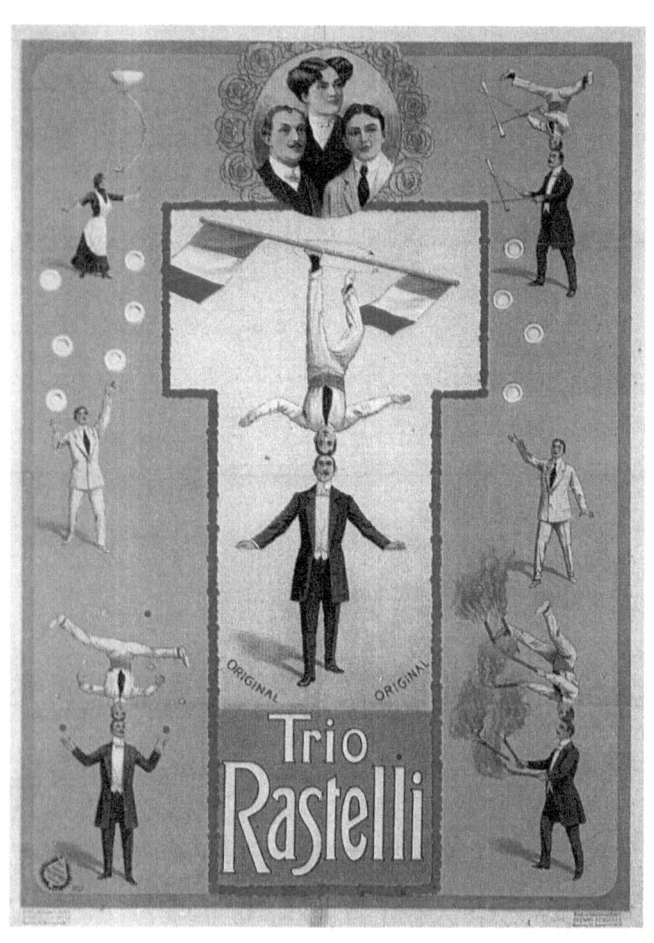

Trio Rastelli

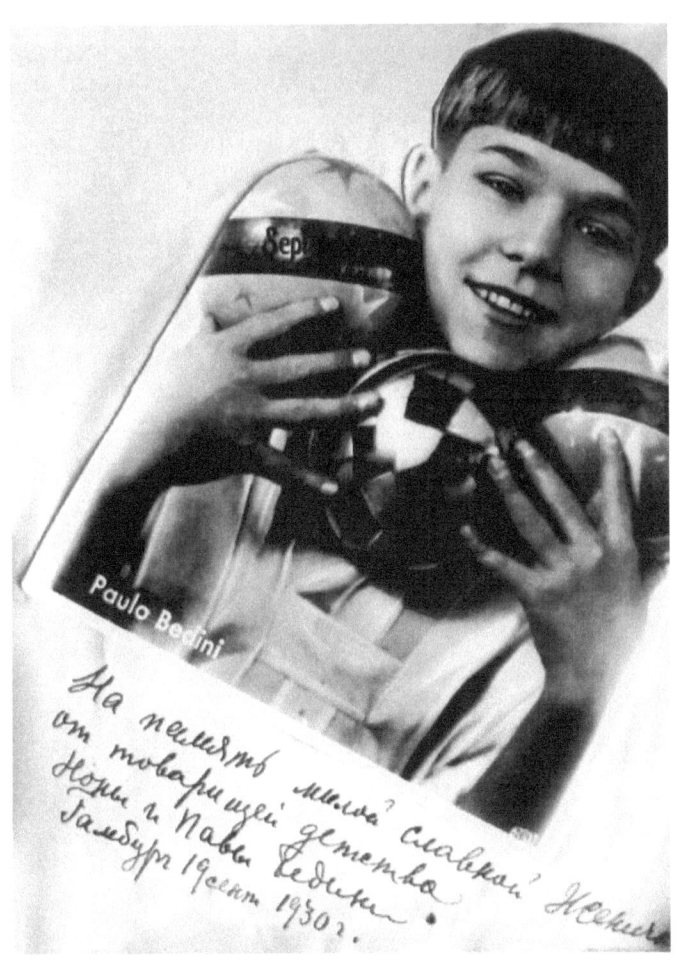

Paulo Bedini

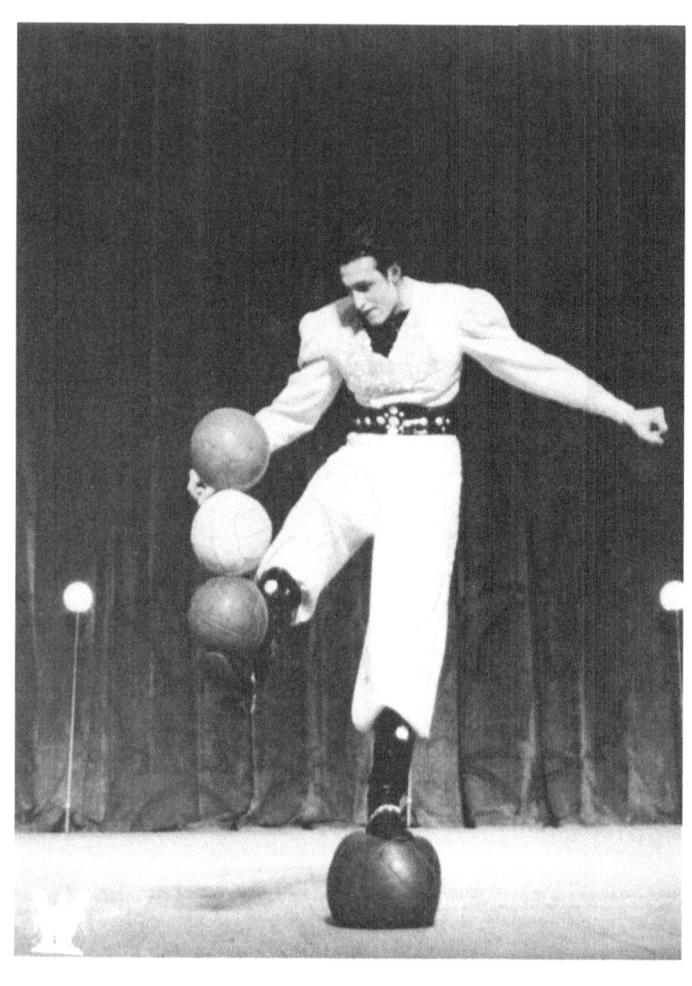

Massimiliano Truzzi

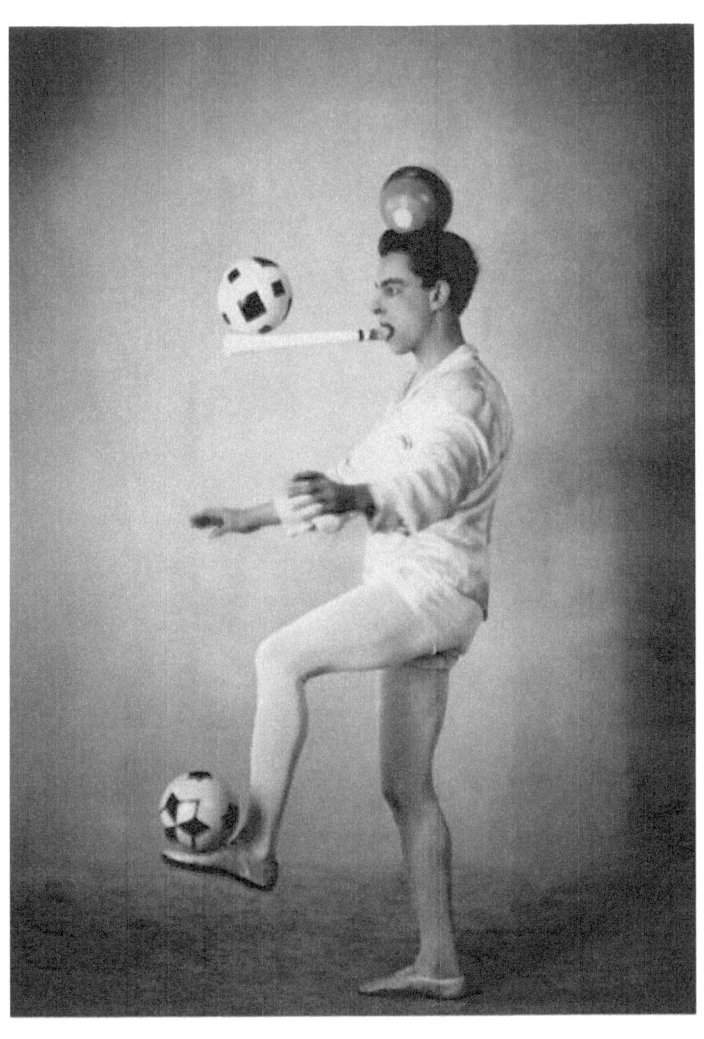

Paolo Piletto

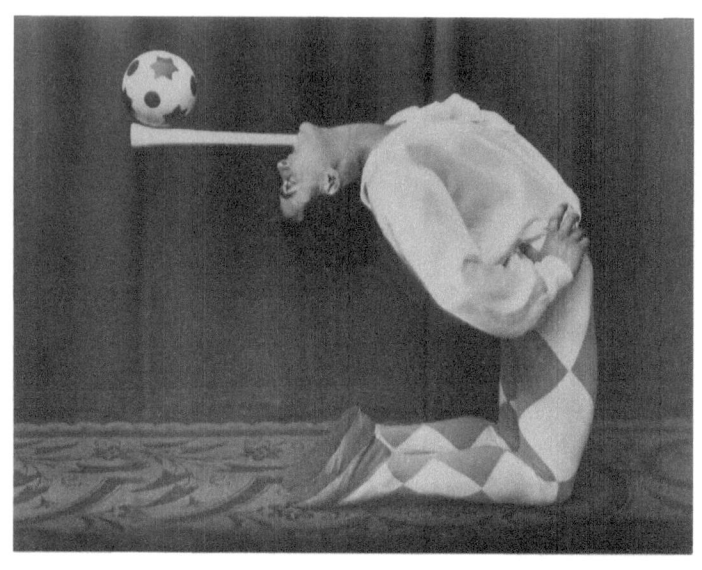

Jean Florian

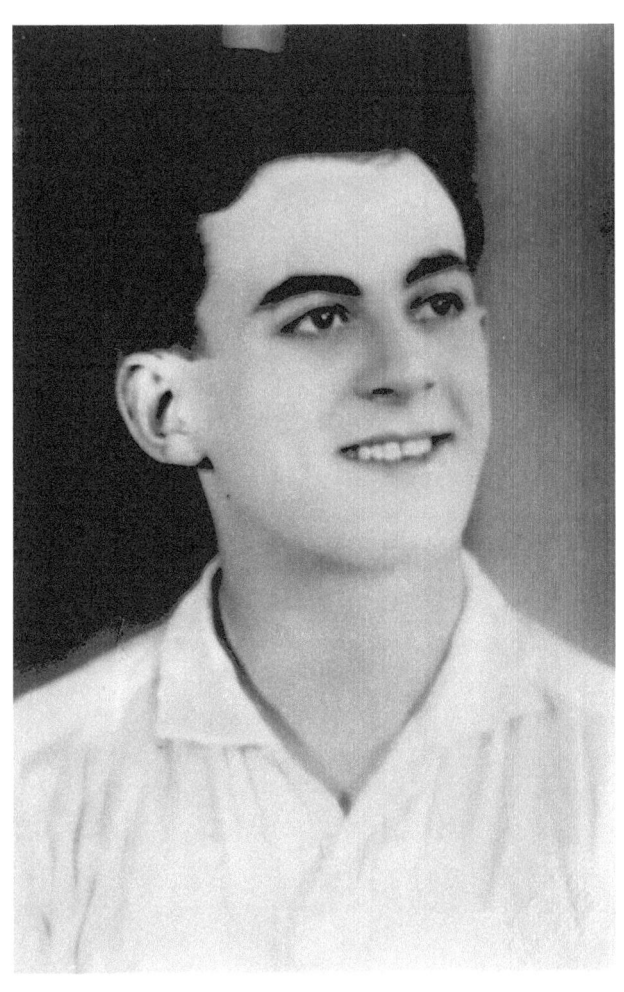

Jean Florian

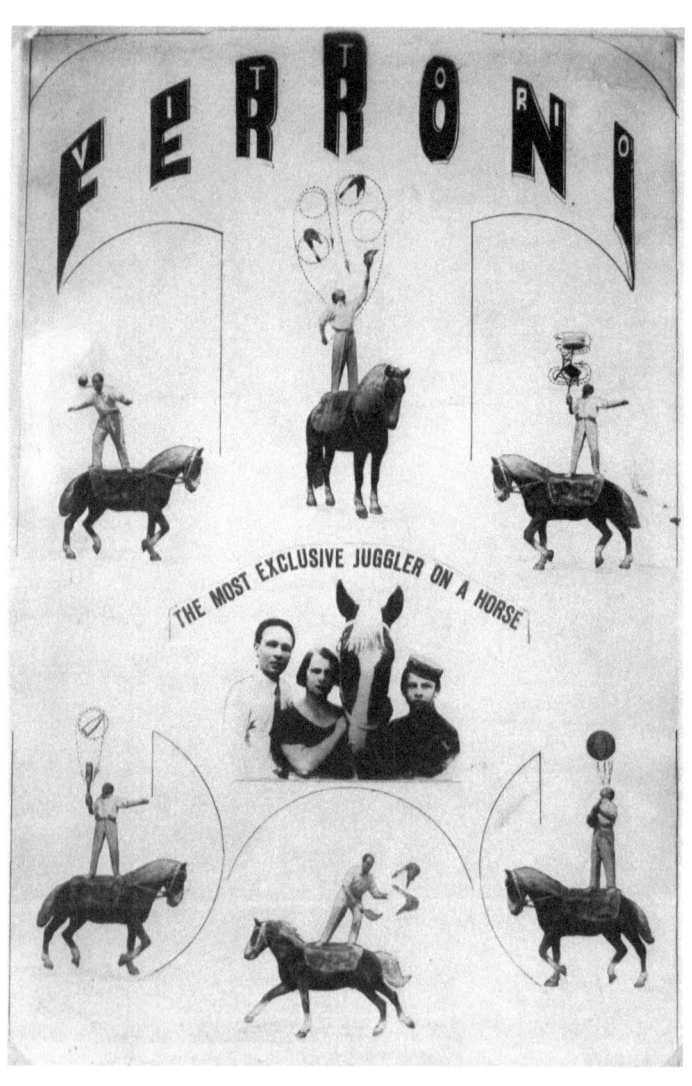

Vittorio (Victor) Ferroni

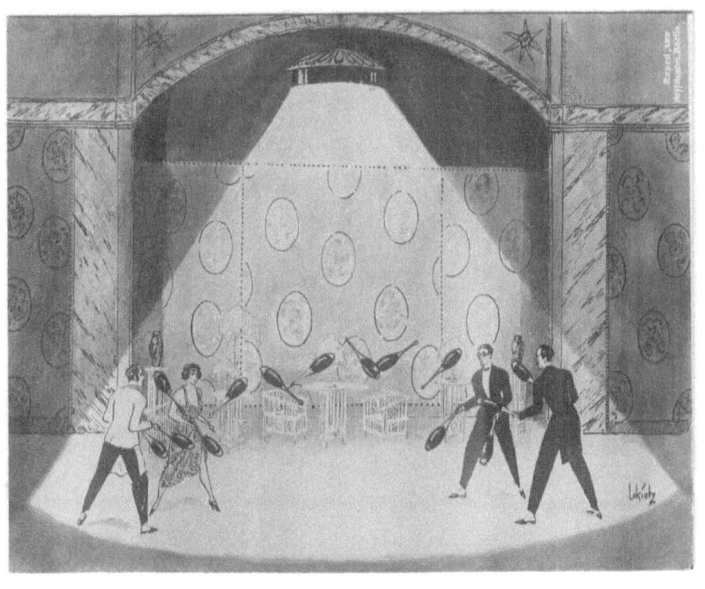

Wallastons

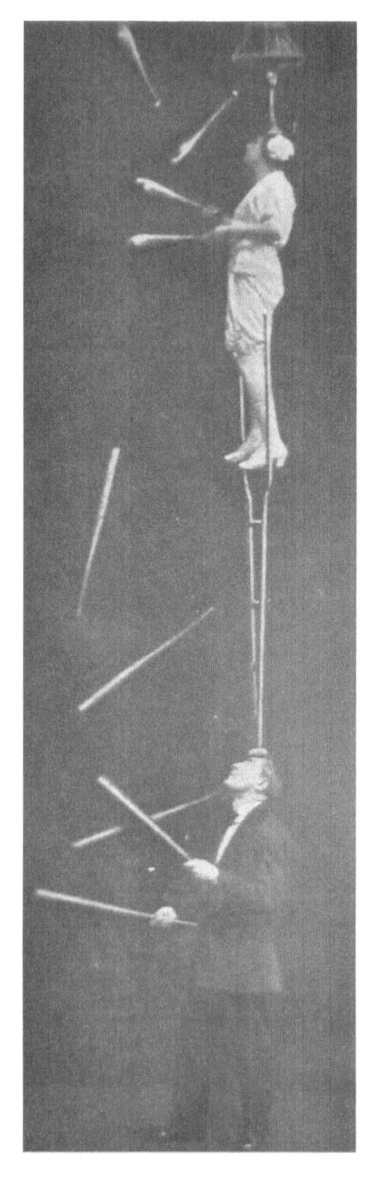

Jospeh Blank

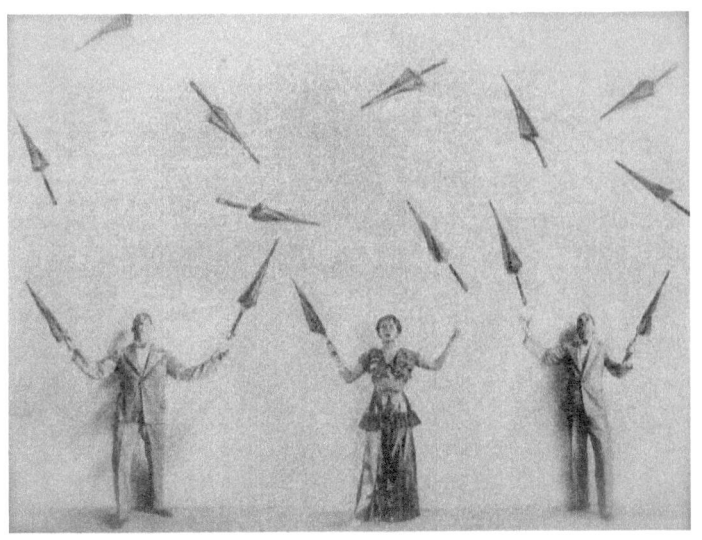

Joseph Blank and partners

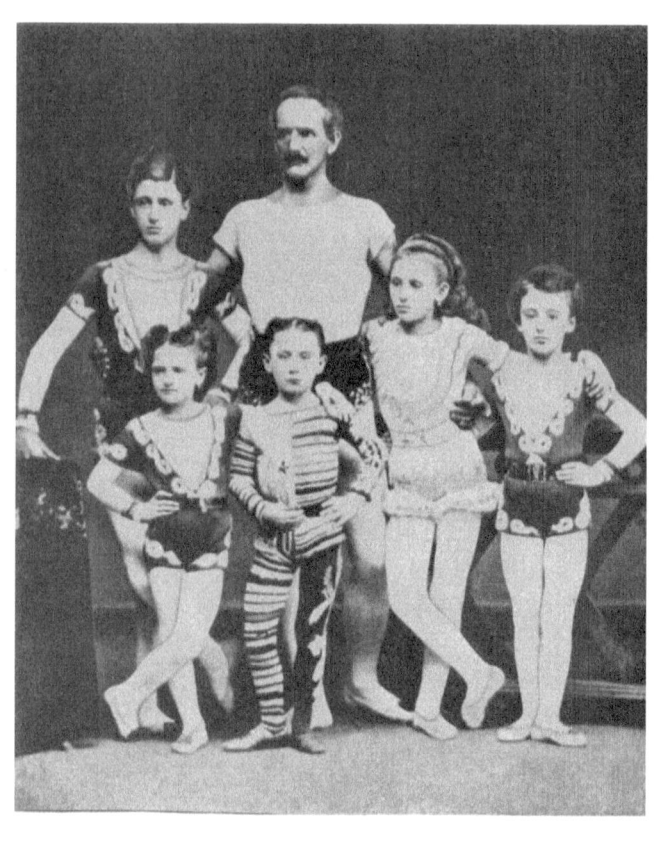

Schäffer family: Karl-Johann, Severus, Sylvester,
Sebaldus, Sidonia, Susanna

APPENDIX

Illustrations from Streli's book
"Acrobatics and Acrobats"

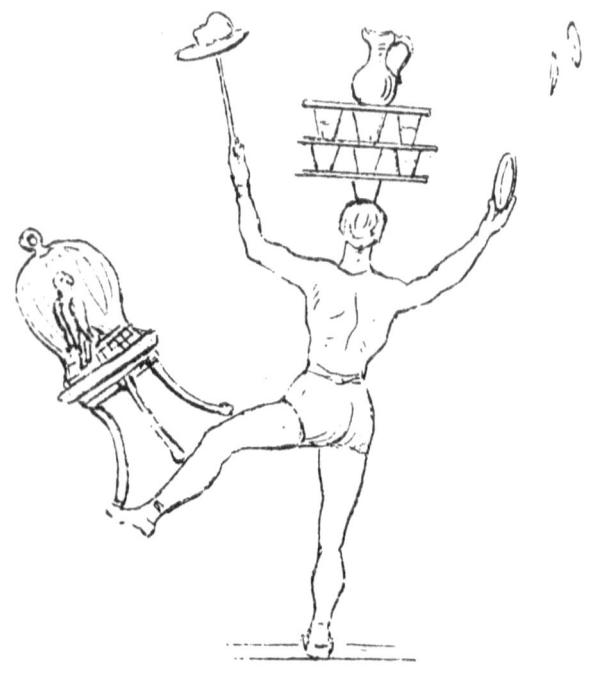

Feat of asymmetric quadruple juggling

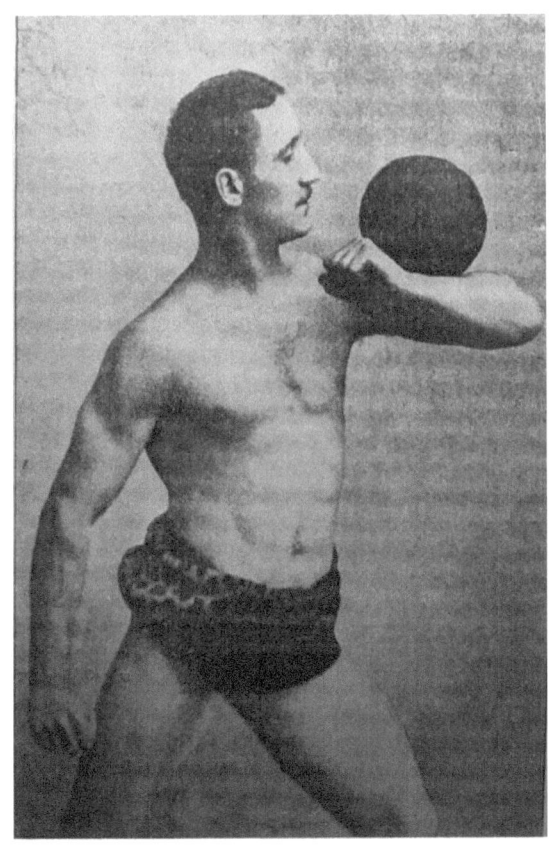

Severus Schäffer

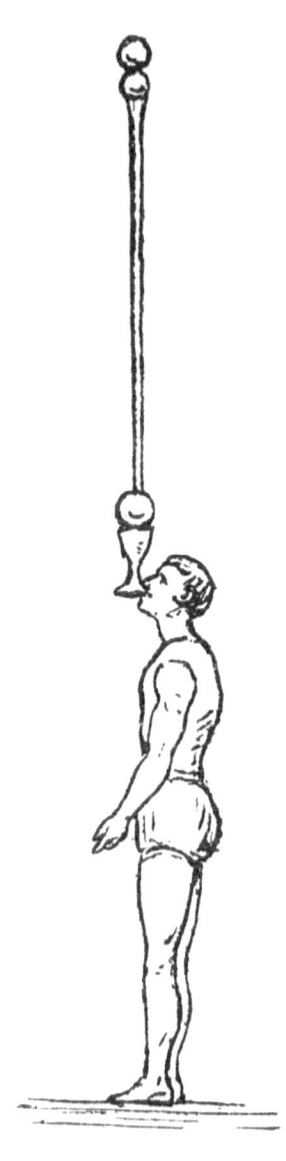

Cinquevalli - Billiard balls and cues

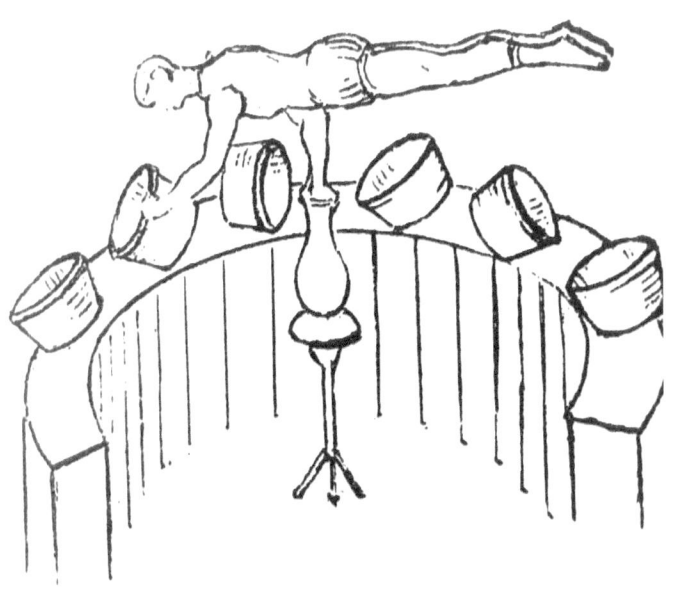

Severus Schäffer - The dancing bowls

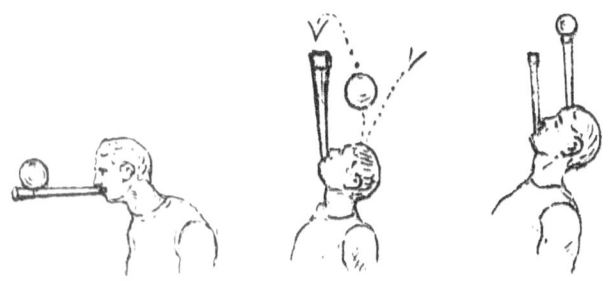

The ball and the mouth stick

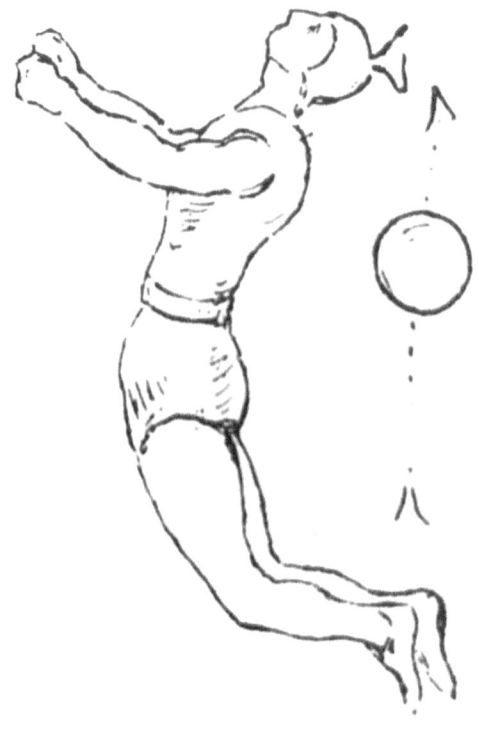

Juggling with a ball

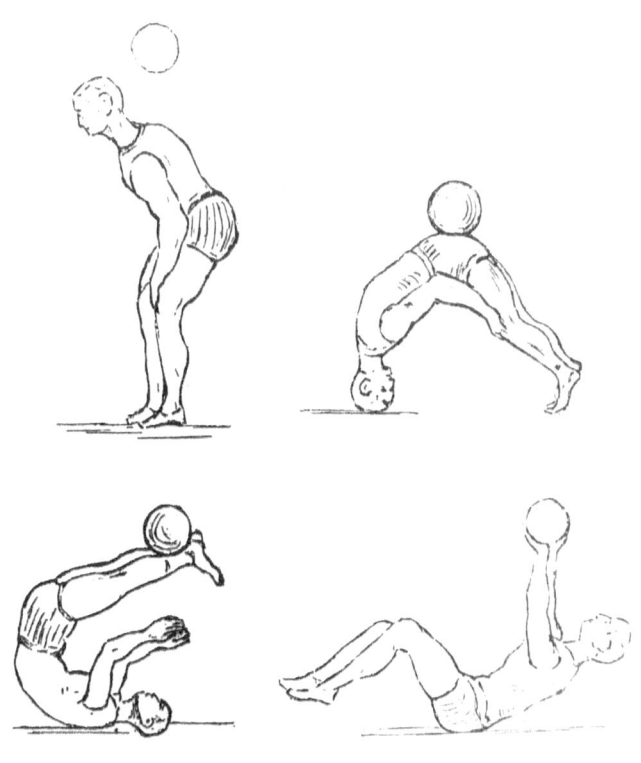

Juggling with a ball by Severus Schäffer

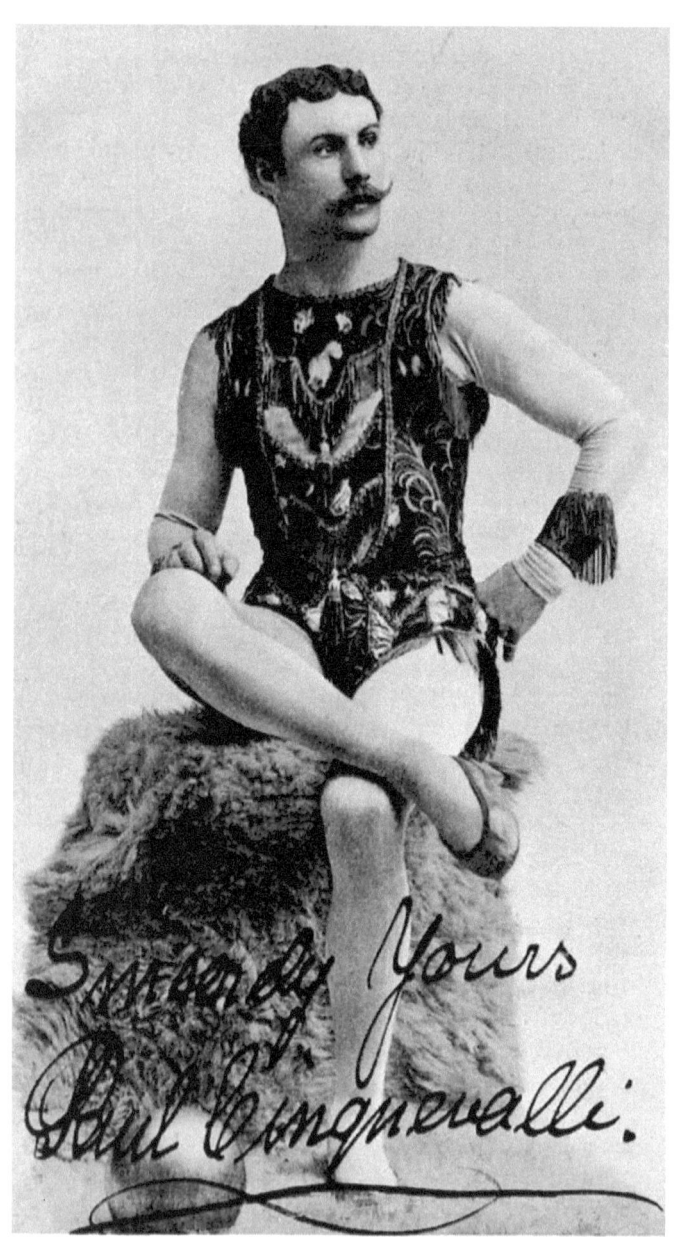

Paul Cinquevalli